THE WAY WE WEREN'T

THE WAY WE WEREN'T

a memoir

■

JILL TALBOT

SOFT SKULL PRESS • AN IMPRINT OF COUNTERPOINT • BERKELEY

LIBRARY OF CONGRESS CATALOGING-IN-PUBLICATION DATA
Talbot, Jill Lynn.
The Way We Weren't : a memoir / Jill Talbot.
pages cm.
ISBN 978-1-59376-615-3 (paperback)
1. Talbot, Jill Lynn. 2. Talbot, Jill Lynn—Relations with men.
3. Talbot, Jill Lynn—Travel—United States. 4. Single mothers—United States—Biography. 5. Mothers and daughters—United States—Biography. 6. Women authors, American—Biography.
7. Loss (Psychology) 8. Creative writing—Psychological aspects. I. Title.

CT275.T215A3 2015
306.874'32092—dc23
[B]

2015007338

Cover Design by Kelly Winton
Interior design by Elyse Strongin, Neuwirth & Associates, Inc.

Soft Skull Press
An Imprint of COUNTERPOINT
2560 Ninth Street, Suite 318
Berkeley, CA 94710
www.softskull.com

Printed in the United States of America
Distributed by Publishers Group West

10 9 8 7 6 5 4 3 2 1

for

INDIE

Always remember that when a man goes out of the room,

he leaves everything in it behind.

When a woman goes out

she carries everything that happened

in the room along with her.

—Alice Munro, Too Much Happiness

PROLOGUE

■

MODIFICATION REQUEST

Stamped Received December 14, 2009
Boulder County Child Support Enforcement Unit

12/07/2009

To Whom It May Concern:

I am writing to you to find resolution regarding modifying child support orders for Indie ███████████ as well as addressing the back child support amount and lifting the suspension on my driver's license.

My situation has changed drastically since the orders were set for child support in 2002.

███████████████████████████████████████
███████████████████████████████████████
███████████████████████████████████████
███████████████████████████████████████
███████████████████████████████████████
███████████████████████████████████████
███████████████████████████████████████
███████████████████████████████████████
███████████████████████████████████████

███████████████████████████   ██

████████████████████

Furthermore, I would like to state for the record that Jill Talbot (the mother of Indie) and I had a short-term relationship with an unexpected pregnancy. I offered to marry Jill and take care of her and Indie. She declined and didn't want anything to do with me. She wanted to move out of state and move on with her life. This was agreeable for both of us. The next time I heard from Jill, she called me in 2003 and asked if I was "happy." I stated that yes I was. She then voiced she wanted nothing from me except to keep my cell phone number the same and let her know if it changed in case she needed to contact me. My cell phone number has always remained the same.

Considering the verbal agreement between Jill and myself, I ceased making payments as I had always struggled to make the child support amount. I moved on with my life and all of a sudden six years later, the issue of child support that we both agreed upon has abruptly resurfaced and I am now $40,000 in debt to her, my driver's license has been suspended, and I am entirely overwhelmed. Dealing with any of these issues could break a person and I need help rectifying this issue quickly so I may focus on my life before it falls apart.

Sincerely,

(3██) 9██-3██

THE MAN IN THE PHOTOGRAPH

She remembers a picture. It's not the one of them drinking and smoking on the patio of the pub, and it's not the one of them shooting pool in the Trailhead Tavern, and it's not the one of her in front of her Jeep on the morning she went back to Texas, knowing with every mile she would eventually turn around and come back for good. It was the picture they asked someone to take of the two of them on that June afternoon.

They had planned a camping trip for the solstice, and while he packed the tent and the sleeping bags, she snuck to the store to get a pregnancy test with dim memories of spending a whole day in May on the blue futon, watching one movie after another. She wishes she could remember what they had been watching, but she was drinking pretty steadily then, her wine consumption at a precarious peak of desperation. What had her so restless with escape, she can write now, might have been what was coming, what was charging toward them with the stealth and threat of a sudden downpour—the two of them who would end up ducking for separate cover.

But that afternoon, a shift in their lives rumbled within her as they drove the hour to Poudre Canyon then stopped at the little store just at the park's entrance. Inside, a dark bar, and a deck out back, where they stood above the roaring river, her in a tank top and shorts and him in a T-shirt, his long plaid shorts. Both of them in flip-flops. Someone took a picture of them: he stood behind her with his arm across her waist, and she leaned back into his large shoulder. And though a stranger held the camera, she's written that it was a man at the bar, a bearded, dark soul of a stranger she cajoled outside with her smile and an offer to buy his next beer. This just one of the scenes she reinvents, again and again, and why not? The man in the photograph is not around to tell her that no, it was not that way at all. His leaving freed her to write the story the way she wishes it to be read. And she's been writing the same story, all these years.

A friend recently asked when she's going to stop, write about something else. Surely he was asking how long until we can let go, move on. How long do we live in the fictions of our past? And how do we convince anyone that who we write is not necessarily who we are?

————————

She receives a letter, the first words in eight years, so she goes searching through closets, suitcases, boxes, and drawers. She can see it, the pewter frame, her sunglasses, the squints in the sun, knows for certain that she keeps it in a box as an answer to a question. It was the picture they put in her nursery, a representation of who they were, who she was, the way the two of them held each other, an assuredness of we. But she cannot find the picture or its pewter frame, the black and white they chose instead of color. Why? Even that afternoon, perhaps, they knew they were already smiling back at who they would, never could, be again. The black and white of a truth it would take her years to see. The truest fiction.

She remembers a box on a high shelf in her closet, one labeled *Pictures*. She goes to the door, opens it, pulls the box down from the highest shelf and peels off the packing tape. And there it is: the frame, the photograph. Him. Her. The sun fighting through clouds, their squinting against the hollows of the canyon, their suspicion that the two of them together would one day be only something she writes about, that they were closer than they knew to a canyon of distance. She stares at the man in the photograph, realizing it is not the man she has been writing for eight years.

It's a story she tells often. One first sentence begins, "He left on a Sunday morning." Or sometimes, she begins, "He left when our daughter was four months old." Still, in every instance, she changes when the story begins: either in those early years in their basement apartment in Fort Collins, or the first summer they met in Vail, or the phone calls she didn't answer in Texas, or the letters he didn't send from Nebraska, or the thrift-store chair where she found him one morning in the seconds before he changed the narrative forever. One thing has remained the same in every version: that he left on a Sunday in September. This is not true. He left on a Saturday in July. Time has become a detail that can change with letters typed on a keyboard, with one click of the delete button.

———————

The photograph frames a memory she has never written, how on that afternoon, while he stood on the bank of the river casting a fly rod, she curled under a tree, pen in hand, and wrote of the separateness. Those words, in a small green note-book, tell the real story: she knew, long before he did, that given the chance, she would leave. And she did, again and again. Whether it was in her Jeep or out the door or with a bottle, she was always leaving him. But when she writes, he's the character who leaves. So she has written a forgiveness, given her character a trait she never possessed. One of loving someone with abandon.

———————

Now she lives ten years and seven states away and moves in rooms that he will never see, utters words he will never hear, laughs often. But in her writing, she is with him again, avoiding an ending that came and went years ago.

COLORADO

1999–2003

■

OFF THE GRID

It's true I left Kenny first. It was the end of the summer we met in Colorado, 1999. I packed up my Jeep and drove back to Lubbock, where I had been living for the past four years earning my doctorate. A professor in my department suddenly resigned, so I was offered the visiting position. I chose to be a professor instead of a waitress, which is what I had been in Vail all summer.

All through that next year, Kenny called often—described moonlit roads and the bend of the Eagle River—repeated attempts to navigate my direction. I taught my classes, read novels, drank at a bar on Nineteenth Street, and picked up the phone in my kitchen less and less. I'd listen to his voice on the machine and delete the message.

Kenny knew from the beginning how I carved a distance between us, and every time it reached its apogee, he'd say, "Jill, I know what you're doing." He could pull me back with the tone of his voice, a few words. But his leavings made up a course that was harder to reverse.

It was as if we were in orbit, taking turns being the sun.

When the spring semester ended that year in Lubbock, I cut my hair short and drove to Colorado. Once there, I passed the exit to Minturn I had taken so many times the previous summer, and I took the one to Avon, where Kenny had moved. I found a pay phone outside a convenience store and dialed the number I had been ignoring for the past year. He picked up and gave me directions up the winding hill to his apartment, a second-floor with a hammock on the balcony, where I spent most days reading while he wired homes in new developments in the Vail Valley. On weekends, we'd sit across from each other on the couch, talking about a Hemingway story he had just read. At night, we'd slide the balcony door open, turn out the lights, and drink beer. As The Band or Van Morrison sang, we watched the clouds. But the summer didn't seem as simple as the one before, and during the deepest part of one of those nights, I got out of bed and went outside. It was a move I would make for years to come, leaving him alone in our bed. That night, I walked to the edge of the complex's property and stood for a long while, staring across the gulch between me and I-70. The moon like a streetlight. Each time a car went by, I wondered if I should get back on that highway.

Years later, Kenny would use this night in arguments. He threw it at me so many times it became like tossing a T-shirt or a dish towel across a room. He'd tell how he woke to find me gone, how he went to the balcony and saw me outside, the outline of my frame in the dark. He'd say that every time he felt me disappearing, that night would come back to him. "I warned myself about loving you," he'd say, more to himself. I never told him the way I felt, as if I were still standing out there trying to redirect the traffic of my doubts.

I remember it feeling like the slow motion of astronauts being pulled away by an invisible force. To Kenny, I am sure, it seemed I would float forever, never truly stay, but I was attached to him like a tether.

In the fall of 2000, I took a job teaching at a community college in Fort Collins. Kenny stayed in Avon, and every weekend, we'd take turns driving the three hours between us on Fridays before turning back on Sundays. During those months, it was too soon to chart our separations as the start of a long series of leavings, both his and mine.

Eventually, Kenny moved into my basement apartment in Fort Collins. After a few months, it was his turn to test the gravity between us, and he left and came back. Twice. And then he went often, working in refineries in faraway states for months at a time. And in his absence, I wrote poems, followed line after line believing, as I would for years, that my words were the way to guide him home. But I was writing myself away more than anything, shuddering at the white spaces—of the weight of something I knew I couldn't bear. That's when I began leaving him in the wine, the nights suspended between a bottle or two.

I was standing out at that edge again, but this time, instead of walking out into the dark, I drank in it. The suspicion I wanted a different life pulling at me with such force, I'd crawl up the steps and out our door to escape it. The tinkling of the wind chime sounded its indifference while

I took deep breaths and fixed my eyes on the moon the way dancers choose a place to spot so that when they turn, again and again, they will not stumble. The rotation of my own axis caught in a dangerous veer. During one of our runs on a January night, I told Kenny I wanted to move, to write, that the lines I had begun in that apartment were like grids, their coordinates fixed. They steadied me.

That spring while I waited to hear from writing programs, something else steadied me: my daughter, Indie. It is difficult to explain the way I knew this, but it felt as if she were coming to save me because my drinking had reached such a level I had begun to leave myself. This time, it was Indie who pulled me back.

When we moved to Boulder so I could study creative writing at the University of Colorado, I was four months pregnant, and after Indie was born, Kenny and I moved from our apartment on Elder Avenue to a third-story apartment in family housing behind the CU football stadium. By the time Indie was four months old, Kenny left for the last time, and I stayed, bound to an unattached tether.

That's when my real leavings began.

WINE LIST

2000 Beringer Founders' Estate Chardonnay $14.99

A green-tinged bottle leans in the refrigerator door. *One glass*, I think, *maybe two*. The wooden arm of our futon as serving table: a glass of Chardonnay and a plate of Gouda, some strawberries. I uncork the wine as the Seattle skyline is traced for *Frasier*. These are the months of reservation, of balance, before the surface tilts too far and the oblique angles of our nights are formed by the second bottle. He tells me the next morning that yes, we did get all the way through *Out of Africa*. Subtle tones with teary, two AM highlights.

2000 La Cana Albarino $14.79

1999 Chateau Ste. Michelle Cabernet Sauvignon $14.95

We go to Adam and Camille's to measure our misgivings against their Neil Young CD collection and Crate & Barrel cutlery. This is the living room where I will wander, three months later, as an answer to this very evening's question, when I'll act as if no predecessor—not liquor, and certainly not love—tongued my lips before an end-of-the-evening port. He will be gone by then. He will come back. Twice in the span of a year. But this night, when we leave after a seared salmon and Shiraz pairing that holds up much stronger than glances in the glare of another couple, I ask him to turn toward the Old Town Liquor Store. Digits on his truck dash already at 9:03, the *OPEN* sign in the window dark, the stacks of Blue Moon cases only shadows. I scream. He tells me my drinking scares him, but I'm not screaming about the liquor store being closed. I'm screaming because he's nothing like Adam. Plenty of complexity, a thoroughly seductive red.

2000 Parducci Merlot   **$10.29**

My glass on the stove holds a currant ellipse while cherry tomatoes simmer. Such slow afternoons that bear his easy absence. Nebraska for two weeks, San Diego for a month, Corpus Christi, Texas for eight weeks. He fits pipe and shoves sleevers in refineries while I creep through the basement of a blue house to fit my longing into lines, shove past lovers into poems. Dangerous work. A reading chair in the bedroom, a writing desk beneath three shelves of books and a boxy stereo. Our calls from phones attached to walls, the spirals taut and bobbing above thin carpet. He whispers across the states, the state of our togetherness never more stable and sure. I sip wine as water boils, the concurrent eruptions of release across our distant rooms. "Hello, sweet man." "Oh, hello, sweet woman." These years, his absence is the hold between us, a cord we cannot cut. Tea-leaf spiciness flavored with shared lust and mint.

2000 Frog's Leap Chardonnay   **$8 (by the glass)**

I choose a corner table on the patio of The Crown Pub. He's gone to fly-fish the Poudre, so I read Alice Munro, solitude. Leaves shuffle across my feet, my blue pen underlining: "You won't feel it every minute, but you won't spend many days without it." It's safe, this allowance to miss him. I flip to the back inside cover, jot down pieces of conversations from nearby tables, this paperback full of fragments: "He said fifth grade was all maraschino cherries and iron-ons." "Maybe if it had been an orange skirt, it would have been different." He surprises me, pulls up a chair and points to my glass, not a question. Signaling the server, he asks about the story I'm reading. My legs propped in his lap, crossed at the ankles as I tell him about the maraschino cherries. Years later, I'll walk by this moment, see the two of us and the glints of more-than-gold in glasses. Hints of agony inside a stilling wind. And one morning, I'll teach Munro from that same copy and turn to the back of the book, wanting to tell my students that the stories we read and the stories we remember are the same. This offering is crisp, with hints of wet stone and yellowed pages.

1997 La Crema Chardonnay $15.99

The blue of our futon splayed out in the living room. Bodies close, bare, his leg propped over mine. I'm reading the last poem in a book by Sharon Olds. He traces the slip behind my knee with the callous at the base of his left thumb, something I insist he do. The wear and rough of his work, the sudden scratch sharp during the fucking, the way he holds himself above as my hands move like opening curtains on his chest. The first time we came together, it was moans spilling down the stairs from the second floor and through the house, the rush of the Eagle River outside the open window. In the poem, the woman looks through her window to the snow just after love. "I cannot see beyond it." My voice catches on the line. They are our words. We have no idea. We cannot see beyond this moment, the blue of the futon, the blue of the book's cover, the blue of my eyes, wet with the shudders of spent thirst. Subtle toasted oak, butterscotch.

2000 Fess Parker Santa Barbara Viognier $20.99

1998 Columbia Crest Chardonnay $11.49

A corner pantry transformed into a closet, a single curtain panel hung across the opening where he keeps his fly-fishing gear, running clothes, the plaid of his shirts, and a used Priority Mail box he keeps taped shut. His clothes hamper—the boxers, the jeans with a hole in the left knee, all the flannel, the crumpled running socks and my gray tank—spills onto the tile floor like a rumor. A solid base of yellow apple fruit with a hint of resentful undertones.

1999 Big House Red $9.99

This will be the beginning of two-bottle nights. His truck pulled up to the back door on a February morning. The tracks from the alley to the back porch, the back and forth of his boot prints, the hamper squeezed between the seat and the back window, where his fly rod case sticks up like a warning before an uneven road. I stand at the back window, ready for him to pull away and drive back to New Mexico. He calls from a bowling alley a few days later, and it is only then, after he has gone enough distance to allow me to keep my own, that I can tell him. It's not time apart. Or time out. Our time is up. It's time. And he hangs up, says he's going back to his sandwich at the bar. I grip the phone for a long time, look out the back window to see his tracks already covered with a heavy, wet snow. This finish lingers, with flavors of vanilla, a hint of rhubarb.

WHAT DOESN'T BREAK LOOSE

She doesn't like the way he sits for hours at her writing desk with his guitar resting on his knee, searching for chord sequences on her computer. She paces behind him, worried he'll find her poems and read the way she writes these rooms. It's as if he's rummaging through drawers, disrupting the order of her lines, the arrangement of words she reads aloud, reassembles, deletes. She sits on the futon behind him, feeling like she's in the room alone. He is focused, lost in lines he's trying to learn, getting a few notes in, beginning again. He drops a chord, and the dissonance from a misplaced finger scratches her impatience, sharpens it.

It's like the tray they have in the drawer by the stove, the one for cutlery, the way he puts forks in with the knives, leaves spoons turned upside down, the way she fishes out paper clips and pencil stubs, a roll of electrical tape from the section for serving pieces. She wants it all to remain intact, untouched. But he has been away, and their languages are distant, separate.

So when he stands, sets the guitar against the wall in the corner, she tells him that the computer, and she points to it, is like his tool belt, something she's never even touched, she doesn't think, because it holds everything he uses to do the things she can't begin to understand, like when she watches him reposition a fixture, unable to comprehend the intricacies of the wires inside the walls. There is too much hidden here, formulated constructions hidden behind the everyday: the phone book on the counter, the green apples in the crisper, the stack of folded laundry on the dresser. What is unsaid, what is unknown like a foundation that has settled unevenly.

He has been on the road for two months—working in the middle of the night in refineries alongside men whose words are rough, blunt—and for the first few days he is back, his language holds no meaning for her. He speaks in platitudes, handfuls of fucks, and her own words feel heavy, as if she bears two overstuffed grocery bags in each hand up the three flights of stairs to their apartment while he carries a single bottle of water.

The next morning, he sits at the kitchen table in his welding cap and overalls, she in her bathrobe and hot-pink slippers. She tells him how their languages screech like boxcars pulling toward one another, her fingers interlacing over the steam of her coffee cup in explanation. She asks him what it's called, when the cars come together, and he says he doesn't know, but it's like a locking of the metal. His hand presses down, palm flat.

Years from now, she will be teaching in a department in Oklahoma with a famous poet, and each time she passes the woman, a diminutive figure who often wears scratchy red skirts and keeps her black hair pulled back tight in a low bun, she will pause without notice, not wanting to disrupt the ordinary—the passing of a colleague in the hallway—with the awe she feels in using the same stairs, standing in front of the same mailboxes, as this woman.

The poet dies. Suddenly. Unexpectedly. A call goes out for volunteers, students, faculty, to help the family move her things from the house on the corner. She calls her colleague, tells him she'll be there in the morning.

When she steps into the living room, she's asked to help catalogue every book in the poet's house, to record every notation, every scribbled sentence. She sits on a wicker couch she recognizes from a poem and picks up one book after another, transcribes the notes in the margins. Such a revealing, she thinks. Beyond the living room, others call from rooms what they have found. As they wander through rooms, she goes searching through pages.

The poet lived alone. She had a few cats and a small desk in the living room, bookcases, stacks of books on tables and along the walls on the floor, some of them her own. She didn't like to fly, didn't have a car, never saw a doctor, kept to herself in that house, so when she went in to the hospital with pneumonia and the doctors found the cancer, she was gone in three days. Such isolation, such refusal, a stubbornness that bore itself out in the vice of her poetry.

For days she sits on this poet's couch, handles every book, every page with care, can't shake the projection of someone sifting through her own books, her own markings, knowing what they would confess. One of the poet's lines keeps coming to her, and she says it to herself like a litany:

Your own life
is a chain of words
that one day will snap.

On the last day, when most of the furniture has been hauled away, and the cats have been adopted by graduate students, and the books are in taped-up boxes, she looks around at the bare walls. Through one doorway, she can see to the light blue stove in the kitchen, and through another, the pressed clothes crammed into an open closet in the bedroom. She realizes if she keeps living the way she is living, making the choices that perpetuate her solitude, she will die a woman alone with her books. For months after, she turns down a street out of her way to drive by the poet's house as if she's trying to figure something out, but she can't decide what, so she decides to stop doing it, to stop staring at an empty house where a famous poet once lived.

———

When he comes home from work that afternoon, he leaves his work boots in the entryway and steps into the kitchen to get out bread and peanut butter. She is still at the computer and turns around in her chair to tell him about a poem she read once about a man caught in between two boxcars, but she can't remember who wrote it. He warns her it's a dangerous job, connecting, that if the worker gets caught in between, it's not until they pry them apart that he dies. She writes the details of her fingers interlacing over the coffee cup. Years from now, she will not be able to recall if there ever was such a morning conversation over coffee or it was just something she wrote.

———

She thinks of the poet's house as a void. A place where a woman locked herself in, locked herself down, lived in her work. Every time she reads her own poem about the boxcars, she returns to the apartment where she wrote it, remembers it as a space of separate rooms, like the two of them, never connecting.

Where we live, our houses, our apartments, reveal how we live, or don't. She is going back. To wander rooms like pages, to find hidden passages, the story, the notes in the margin. To the house in Utah, the duplex in Oklahoma, the motel in Montana, the two-story in New York, to places where she has lived. And left.

CEDAR CITY, UTAH

2003–2006

∎

STALLED

I like to live on corners, to position myself at the intersection of directions and indecisions. I understand repetition, ritual, the pause before going on, passing through. I even understand turning around and going back, again. Like the way I've already written about that house in Utah, but I've left something out and need to go back to it again, where I will find myself answering a phone call.

It is the end of July, and I'm in the middle of the floor next to the crib, waiting to hear the slowed rhythm of Indie's breaths. She shifts in the crib, fights sleep. The tiny lamp on in the corner, the glow in the room a whisper. I stretch out on my back, look up at the ceiling, the slats of wood painted wide. I rented this house over the phone when the landlord told me it was on the corner. I told him I'd send the deposit that afternoon.

From the window of the room, I can see the garden of the elderly woman who lives next door. A blue truck sits in front of her house, always parked at the curb. It was her husband's truck. He has been dead for a year.

I once bought Kenny a blue truck with money I won from a writing contest. And I watched for that truck's lights to pull into the parking lot from a third-floor window in Boulder those nights he wouldn't come home. For months after that truck pulled away on a Sunday morning, my breath caught if I ever passed or pulled up behind a truck that shade of blue. When I moved to the house in Utah and saw a blue truck parked next door, I kept expecting to see to it pull away. But weeks passed. It never moved. When a neighbor told me it belonged to the man who lived next door for fifty-six years before dying in April, I could afford the stasis, understood the metonymy of a blue truck.

In that house in Utah, I wrote at the same desk that fit below the bookshelf in the basement apartment where Kenny and I lived together in Fort Collins, the desk that overlooked the river outside our spare bedroom in Boulder, the desk in the corner of our living room in the last apartment we shared.

During those three years in Utah, I never found a good place for the desk. I'd slide it from the window to the side wall in the front room, and eventually, I dragged it by a window in my bedroom. Then I moved it to an opposite wall. That's the last place I remember it being. When I wrote there, I'd get up from the desk mid-paragraph and wander into the living room, stand at the front window and watch the rain. Thinking of the next line. Thinking of Kenny.

———

When I hear the eased rhythm of Indie's breathing, I stand up slowly, in case this is not sleep, in case it's just the moment before, when the slightest move will cause her to stir, sit up. If she wakes, the winding down must start all over. It's like runners who get halfway down the track before being called back because of a false start. When I see her arms above her head in surrender, I take slow steps out of the room and toward the kitchen to begin my evening.

I pull the heavy bottle of Chardonnay from the bottom shelf of the refrigerator. As the night dissolves, I pour glass after glass, empty a bottle, uncork another. Eventually, I move to the front porch with my glass and the bottle, assume my nightly position on the top step, where I'll be stalled until three AM. I know it will be three because that's when the automatic sprinklers turn on in the front yard. I watch the streams crisscross the lawn, the sidewalks darken. Across the yard in the dark, the blue truck is a shadow. At some point, I go into the house to get my phone, but I won't remember this.

———

Several months after Kenny moved out of our apartment in Boulder, he called me from a motel room, somewhere in Colorado, but he wouldn't say where. He told me he had driven until he felt far enough away to see if distance could make his decision. I had not known until that night he wasn't gone all the way, that there was the chance he might return. He told me he was sitting in a chair, and he was going to stay there all night and feel which way his heart pulled. Toward me or the woman I saw only once, walking down a sidewalk. I willed myself to reach through all the distant towns and dark highways and find him in that chair, wherever it was, and pull him home. But he didn't come back, and he didn't stop calling, so the two of us stayed at the intersection of his indecision. Even after I drove myself west to Utah, to live, it still wasn't enough distance.

One afternoon, I opened the top drawer of my writing desk and felt a heavy shift, watched the drawers of the right side collapse. I stood back to accept what seemed a fitting end. Then I took all the papers, postcards, and envelopes, all the pictures from each drawer. With each removal, another piece of the desk loosened, broke free. Nothing within me shifted.

One night long after that, Kenny called from a bar to tell me someone had just chosen "Please Come to Boston" on the jukebox. I could hear it through the phone. Our song, the one about asking someone to come to Boston for the springtime, to Denver with the snowfall, to L.A. to live forever. I knew every word, but I had no way to follow this new song he had started singing, the one with the part about calling me during the day, asking how I liked the new town, if a television station showed *Frasier* at ten thirty the way it did in Colorado when I'd watch it every night. He told me it comforted him, knowing where I was every night at ten thirty. I knew he was not bound to rituals the way I was, so I had no way of grounding him in any place, at any time. Please come to Utah. He just said no.

But that's not the phone call I always hear myself answering. It's the one the morning after the night I went back into the house to grab my phone, the call I didn't remember making.

The phone is ringing, and I look at the number and see that it's his. In that instant, a scene from the night: sprinklers running and me speaking into the phone, spilling myself all over the steps of the porch and out to the yard with my longing.

The sun in my room like a neighbor who witnessed the whole thing through parted drapes, and I wince at what I might have said in the middle of the night, in the middle of the second bottle. It feels like I'm in the middle of nowhere, as if all the directions I have ever written down are wrong. I wonder if he is about to tell me he's on his way to Utah, on his way to us. I press the green button to answer. Press my other hand to my heavy head. Yesterday I turned thirty-three. Nothing has changed or feels like it ever will.

When he says, "Jill," it is stern, angry, the voice he uses when someone else is in the room. I understand my message has been listened to, but not by him. I assure him that no, I will not call again. Yes, I understand I cannot do this anymore. And then he says what I never needed to hear, that he loves the woman who is in the room.

Indie's muffled cries begin, and they grow louder as she comes out of sleep. I tell Kenny I have to go, and that I will not bother him anymore. When he says good-bye, I note a shift in his voice. I know I will always remember it as the last day of July, the first day of my thirty-third year, five months into Indie's second, and the last day Kenny lived halfway between me and another woman.

DARK

When she thinks about her house in Utah, she's always standing at the kitchen window looking out to the grass between the house and the street. That window may have had curtains for the three years she lived there, but she doesn't remember. Maybe they were a blue-checkered pattern or a thin white sheer, but they've been pulled back in her memory, and all she sees is what's in the frame.

She does remember the small movie theater in town, the screen with a tear in its upper left corner. While she'd wait for the lights to dissolve, she'd stare at the blank screen's flaw, worried it would distract her. But soon the dark would close like a curtain, and she'd forget about it.

It's always the middle of the night at that house in Utah for her, those hours when she'd lean against the light green countertop, a glass of Chardonnay in her hand. She'd stare at the trees lining the edge of the property, the porch light on at the house next door. It would be the darkest part of the evening—seven hours into the wine—the night suspended between her grip on the glass and her grip on the phone.

She saw *Lost in Translation* in that theater. Twice. She remembers how the man whispers to the woman on the street, how grateful she was she couldn't hear what he said. There are words no one else is meant to hear.

Some nights the wine would wear her down, and she'd sob against his absence. The weight in the house so heavy she'd have to open the front door and the windows and wander down the steps to the sidewalk. Then she'd stand there waiting—as if the night might pour another blue truck onto her street. On the next corner, the traffic light would blink through its colors for no one. She'd turn around and go back inside.

And then one night, she stood in the kitchen, barefoot, staring out, suspecting that if she could rupture the walls of her longing, she could escape them. She thought how it had been two years since he left, and still she carried all the words he had said to her through every action: every load of laundry, every page read on the couch, every stroke of mascara in the mirror, and every pouring—one glass after another. She became angry—at his leaving, at his staying, at the way she had brought him to this house in a city he had never seen. She imagined him sleeping in a distant, unknown room while she stayed up night after night, wondering when the missing might end, if it ever would.

She felt as fragile as her favorite glass—the one with a chip in the stem—a foundation so precarious the slightest pressure or setting down would leave her in shards. But it wasn't that she needed to break—that happened the morning he told her he was leaving. And now all the rooms of that house on the corner were scattered with the pieces. She'd wander into her bedroom, open the hall closet, sit in the rocking chair next to her daughter's crib, or turn on the bathroom light and see them. Then she'd pick them up and trace each unpredictable edge under the lights until the wine dissolved them.

That night, the wine. It lead her down a dark aisle. She no longer wanted to wander out to stand, absently, in the middle of the sidewalk, so she flung open the front door and bounded down the three steps of the porch. She stepped toward the lawn on the side of the house until she stood in the middle of it, feeling as if she were entering the very scene she watched every night. She drew back her arm, the glass of wine still in her hand. Standing that way for a long moment as if in a film still, she thought of all she wanted to shatter: missing a man who was, and had been, gone; believing enough words left on a voicemail would be just that, enough; feeling as if a ghost lurked in every room of her house, and she was the one who called it from its corners, demanding it show itself.

She hurled that glass as hard as she could against the bricks, and it exploded in every direction. Pieces scattered, the back-splash of wine on her feet. In the light from the porch next door, she saw the shadow of the base, its jagged stem rising from the grass. The traffic light behind her changed.

When she thinks about this moment, it seems she did this more than once, that there were many nights of throwing glasses at brick walls. Probably because every time she stepped outside, she'd find a shard of glass on the sidewalk between the house and the yard, or she'd catch a sliver imbedded between the blades. She carried each one to the trash to hide any evidence she had once thrown, with force, a full glass of wine against her house in the middle of the night. But it was more than that, more than a private act of outrage or a drunken act of having enough after having too much. That night, she broke *through*. Though she's still not sure, even ten years removed from that night, that she ever really lived in that corner house. She thinks of it more as wandering through rooms with the ghost that turned out to be herself.

Maybe that's why the moment comes back to her again and again, the time she made a tear in the fabric of the night.

AUTOBIOGRAPHIES

When I was in second grade, my teacher, Mrs. Croft, had us each write an autobiography. She told us to add our addresses at the bottom, then roll them up and tie them each to a red balloon. That way, she said, someone might find them and write back. After lunch, we walked out to the large field by the school with our balloons in hand. At Mrs. Croft's count of three, we let them go. I can still see those red balloons floating up and away. I watched mine until I could no longer see it in the sky.

———

Thirty years later, I entered a rehabilitation facility outside Salt Lake City, Utah. We called it The Ridge. While I was there, Indie stayed with a family that had all but taken us both in as their own in Cedar City. I entered The Ridge on December 9 and began a four-day medical detox, which turned most of us into sleeping lumps beneath blankets in dark rooms. Our first task was to write our autobiographies detailing how we got there. The autobiographies were our way of coming clean, so to speak. They told us that if we didn't work through whatever instigated our addictions, we'd go right back to the bottle, the pipe, the pills. They called it "cognitive therapy": read and write your way to a sober new you. To most of the people in The Ridge, a writing assignment was punishment, so it came with a privilege: to go outside. This was enough motivation for most, as the only chance we had to step outside was during the two thirty-minute breaks we got between meetings that began every day at 7:15 AM and lasted until 9:00 PM. And even then, we were supervised.

I had been writing and publishing essays for years, even had a job at a university in the southern part of the state teaching students how to write them, but it wasn't until I went to The Ridge that I learned to stop hiding behind my own lies. Lines.

Since we were separated into groups by a counselor, I didn't get to hear everyone's autobiographies, so in the evenings, I'd sit on one of the couches in the TV lounge and read the ones I missed. It was like being in a workshop, but one in which no one thought about the writing. The words were confessing. The words were admitting. And it made the writing immediate, raw, real.

No one in that place except me and one other guy had been to college. I don't count the college dean because she only lasted two days. Maybe she was too ashamed to stay. Maybe she couldn't do without her Vicodin. Most of the patients were railroad workers, farmers, or rich, bored wives. Most had no job at all—the booze or the crystal meth made sure of that. The only patients who read on a regular basis were me and a twenty-two-year-old bartender.

The bartender woke up in the hospital and was told he had passed out with a gun in his hand, a plan voided by a pint of vodka. Lanky, dark hair, droopy brown eyes. Now he'd be described as James Francoesque, but then, he was the guy who liked to read. David Sedaris, Chuck Palahniuk, James Frey— he'd finish one, bring it down to my room. The small lounge across from the nurse's station had a bookcase, loosely filled with mostly self-help and Michael Crichton, John Grisham, one surprising Joyce Carol Oates, so his girlfriend brought our requested copies twice a week: Cormac McCarthy, Richard Brautigan, Raymond Carver's *Where I'm Calling From*, because we both appreciated irony. But we were there to write our own stories, detail every drink, the damages that had led us to the same exact spot, even on the same day, when we sat on a bench in early December, me drunk, him discharged from the hospital. That day, I stepped behind a glass door, then turned back once more in hopes that I could be let out, that it was all someone else's narrative. He'd be locked up behind a steel door after his shoelaces and the string inside his waistband had been taken from him. His drinking had come on fast, his reluctance toward his intellect its trigger, his final insistence on an artistic portrait of the disgruntled young man, a bottle of vodka, and a gun stolen from behind the bar. He woke up angry, embarrassed, felt like he was living the life he had failed to end. The last I heard, he went back to the bar for the afternoon shift, hoping, like some guy out of a Hemingway story, that it wouldn't be as hard in the daylight.

———————

One of the meth addicts had become so paranoid he moved into the workshop behind his house. He'd peek through the blinds, watching his wife and two teenage sons as they came and went from the grocery store or school. Then he watched them move out.

———————

My counselor's last words to me on the day I checked out: "You don't have to be Hemingway to be a writer. You don't have to drink or be sad."

They'd often tell us that the sobriety rate for people leaving rehab was 10 percent, so that out of the thirty or so of us in there at any given time, three would stay sober. The rest of us would go back to drinking or drugs, or we would eventually develop some cross addiction. If we had been drinkers, we might turn to pills. Or pills might be replaced by cocaine. Cocaine by booze. It was a trick addicts played on themselves, they'd say, kicking a habit while forming a new one. They'd also warn that if we kept doing what we had been doing, we'd be dead. Some of us soon, because we had already done so much damage that "one more drink" would be too many.

What I had been doing was drinking Chardonnay, as early as ten in the morning on some days and as late as three in the morning some nights. I had loved Kenny for years, and then he suddenly left me and our daughter, Indie, when she was only four and a half months old. He abandoned us. But I abandoned us, too.

———

A blackjack dealer had worked downtown Las Vegas at the Four Queens during its opening years, her cans of Bud and a Camel as quick as the cards. The doctors said her liver was in pieces, shards, really. Most of the time, she slept in her room, a vaporizer belching loudly beside her bed at all hours, her door propped open, the room dark even in the day, her frailty a shadow beneath intricate afghans and a green sleeping bag. She wasn't strong enough to walk, so we took turns bringing her meals on trays or holding her arm as she shuffled to the TV room. Once, someone found her on the smoking patio, her fingers fumbling to light a cigarette. Such futility, no more damage to be done. She was not well enough to attend sessions on schedule, and when she did, her head lolled to the side in sleep, her body bundled in that purple robe. She never wrote her autobiography. Either she couldn't remember it, or it didn't matter anymore. When the coughs smothered her, we'd all look down at the floor or our notebooks, offering her the only form of privacy possible in a circle of people who saw her as a cautionary tale. At sixty, she looked eighty. Her raspiness, her weightlessness an ugly whisper from a fast life that not one of us envied. She had been there at the beginning, she said, one of the invisibles shuffling blind in the lights of the casinos. "I kept a can of Bud right there at the table," she told me once. We regretted it for her, all of it. The last I heard, her husband showed up, belligerent, demanding to know just how long she had been there before taking her home.

———

Being locked up in the rooms of a rehab facility for twenty-eight days, certain phrases got repeated until it was just noise, a skipping record: "Fake it till you make it." "It works if you work it." "Work as hard for your recovery as you did for your addiction." "You're only as sick as your secrets." The head counselor's favorite: "Don't sympathize. Empathize." He'd explain, at least once a day, that when people read their auto-biographies or shared in a meeting, we were not to feel sorry for them. We were to understand, to share the experience, not distance ourselves with pity. The stories we heard were ours. Or they would be if we weren't careful.

———

A man checked out. He showed up two days later on the bench by the nurse's station. He had been badly beaten, or worse. Someone whispered about a liter of whiskey, a night in the ER, but we never got to ask him. They locked him up in the psych ward.

One guy who left The Ridge on the day I arrived hung himself a week later.

My roommate took only two days at home before a bender ended with a mess of police cars in the front yard of her Park City home. Before The Ridge, she had done two stints at Betty Ford.

One man died within a month. Sober. He died from all the drinking he had already done.

One man disappeared.

Five months after I left The Ridge, I made it to the end of the spring semester before I drove to the next town, got a hotel room, then spent the rest of the evening at the bar, convinced that if I didn't drink at home, it didn't count. It wasn't a cross addiction; it was cross location.

———————

One of the railroad men had snorted coke on the long runs in the middle of the night. He chewed on plastic flossers during meetings and wore a University of Texas baseball cap backwards, even though he was fifty. One night, I sat with him alone in the room where we usually played Scattergories. The room had one window, an elongated table, worn plastic chairs, a closet with extra blankets and plastic sheets. He was stuck at Step 1, the autobiography phase, staring for weeks at a blank page and a pen that would not take his disappointment, the guilt. So I sat across from him and asked questions about her, the worst nights, their recent phone exchanges, and wrote it all down. I asked until he had no more answers, so I wrote the rest of the questions and then pushed the yellow legal pad across the table. I ducked out of the room, leaving him to stare at the vocabulary of his failings. He claimed to be friends with a famous author, a woman who, according to him, had a framed picture of his chest X-ray prominently displayed in her living room next to a couple of hanging plants. He liked to draw spirals on the pages of my notebook during meetings. Once, during a session on dream analysis, he told about standing in the middle of a diving board. The psychiatrist on staff preferred Jung, told him that the board was an archetypal symbol of both risk and abandon. After we both left, we spoke on the phone once, me in my kitchen in Utah, he on his cell phone on a railcar somewhere across Oregon. The last I heard was his message on my voice mail, "I'm going to die here, but not before I see you first."

A train track ran adjacent to the hospital. I'd stand on that porch watching the lights of the passing cars and think about scaling the wall and hopping one. One night during a smoke break, one of the psychiatrists came out to the patio looking for me. He said he wanted to meet the professor who drank a gallon of wine every night. "You," he said, slapping my back, "are a legend." I said thank you, crushed out my cigarette, and walked back inside.

When Christmas approached, the counselors told those of us who had been there long enough to progress through our program that we could have a two-hour pass to leave the property and have dinner with friends or family. I used one of my ten-minute phone calls to tell Indie and made plans for someone in the family to drive her the three hours to Salt Lake City so that she and I could have dinner together on Christmas Day.

But hours later, the head counselor called me into his office to tell me I wouldn't be getting a pass, that I still seemed "hell-bent" on running my own program, not theirs, and I wasn't going anywhere. He did, however, give me permission to have Indie visit, though I hesitated. After all, she was only three, and I had told her I was teaching at a "special school" that required me to stay for the month I taught there.

On Christmas afternoon, I stood at the front window, supervised by a staffer, waiting. I saw my white Ford Escape pull up and one of the family's daughters step out of it, and then there was Indie, running full speed down the sidewalk toward the door in a red dress, her blonde hair curly and bouncing, a gift in her hand. When this image comes back to me, as it often does, I shake my head in an attempt to erase it, to never again have to see the little girl excitedly running for the mother who is locked up and not allowed to leave.

The gift Indie gave me that day was a framed piece of red construction paper with scribbles on it. When I asked her what it said, she leaned against me and pointed to the red paper.

"Please come home."

————

Every morning after breakfast, we'd line up at the Nurse's Station for our meds and blood pressure check. In the afternoon, we'd do it again. The girl who cut herself was on an antipsychotic drug. The hay farmer cussed and called everyone a "yahoo" before they took him off Prozac. After a weekend pass to visit her son at home, my roommate returned sedate and peaceful, nothing like the weeping, neurotic beauty she had been in the three weeks I knew her. Once when she was out of the room, I opened the top drawer of her nightstand and found three pill bottles and a cell phone. Contraband. I kept her secret, allowed the counselors to believe "she finally got it." One woman was on something that made her so drowsy she couldn't stay awake during meetings, a rule breaker. And the nineteen-year-old who had been sleeping in the backs of cars on the streets of Salt Lake City tried to charm the staff into giving him "something more." I stepped up to the window and looked down at the tray. The nurse held a white cup with two red capsules. I asked if I could stop taking them. She said she'd bring it up at the staff meeting.

"Not a chance," my counselor told me.

———

I don't remember if any of the students in Mrs. Croft's 1977 second-grade class ever received a letter from our balloon assignment. The balloons probably ended up popped or wilted, found by a stranger who had no idea there had been words. Most likely, in the panhandle of West Texas, they drifted into the middle of some field where the blades of a tractor shredded them. I kept all the pages I wrote from rehab. The fourteen pages of my autobiography, front and back, the notebook pages I drew spirals on during meetings, the pages from the Vietnam vet.

He had worked the rail yards in Portland for seventeen years. He was heavyset, always in jeans and a shirt that struggled around his middle. When he sat down, he'd pull at it, this way and that, trying to get comfortable. He had gotten sober before and it stuck for thirteen years until he took some "stuff that blew his head off." He often fell into coughing fits during meetings and had to step outside for a drink, which was against the rules. He'd shuffle back in, apologize, shake his head at his inability to get through an hour without breaking down. He had dropped out of school. Listening to him read was like watching a man dare the frail of a rope bridge. On one of the last days he was there, he came to the door of the TV lounge and asked if I'd help him with something. We went out to the smoking porch, where he pulled out a form and asked me to write down what he told me. He pointed to the four lines provided beneath the section titled *Addiction History*. "Began using alcohol at the age of fifteen. Pot usage. Meth. Went to AA but stopped going to meetings. Thirteen years of sobriety. Relapse. Three years without alcohol. Came to The Ridge." I pushed the form across the table. He looked at the words as if they were details in a photograph he couldn't quite make out.

It seems strange to feel inferior to someone's pain, to the levels of their addiction, but I always I felt I hadn't done near enough to be locked up with the others. I hadn't lost my daughter. Or my home. Or my job. I hadn't lived on the streets. Or gone to jail. I didn't even have a DUI, which seemed to be a prerequisite. Hearing such autobiographies made me feel one of two ways: either I had no reason to drink, or I hadn't gone far enough with my drinking. I worried I was destined to return. Maybe it would take two years, or five, and I'd be back in the circle, reading a much more disturbing autobiography than Sunday-morning Chardonnay.

Another thing: they always told us we wouldn't stay in touch. We didn't believe them. I didn't believe them. I was wrong. I have no idea where any of those people are—if they're sober, if they're alive.

Once we left The Ridge, we were like balloons released into the air.

AN ITINERANT YEAR
{ Part 1 }

SUMMER 2006

BEGIN

She takes I-15 North and stays on it through Salt Lake City into eastern Idaho. The crowded ranges of Utah's northern mountains give way to the grassy plateaus of southeastern Idaho, and she feels as if she's falling into distance. She drives through a wilderness of trees, those waves of lines cutting through the spacious fields, the low mountain ranges curving at the edges of the horizon, the blue sky set with clouds. She feels herself open up in a state where she has never been. These are slower, deeper breaths.

In Utah, she had a student, a young woman who wrote about the black ice on the highway in New Mexico that took her father. The girl wrote in short lines, dyed her hair deep black and wore red patent heels, wrote about men who were missing: the father who drank himself in and out of rehab and the boy who called himself a robot and would not let her love him. One in a cemetery outside of town, the other sitting next to her in class, both of them recurring characters in her work.

She understood this girl, her writing, the way she unraveled herself because of men who wouldn't stay. The girl liked to take long drives, to roll down the windows, go missing. Far enough to find the signs she needed to read, the ones on the far routes in the empty spaces of southern Utah, the ones that read *BEGIN*. The girl took dozens of pictures of these signs and gave one to her when the class was over.

She keeps it on the refrigerator of every place she lives. A reminder.

She left that house on the corner, all of its rooms empty, every door and set of blinds open. She left pennies, one where her writing desk collapsed, one in the bottom shelf of the refrigerator door, one in the corner of the closet in the front room. And her daughter, by then four, placed one in her own room. The pennies an offering, so the next tenants might have better luck there. On the day they left, the landlord stood in the living room writing a check on the fireplace mantel. Her deposit, all of it returned. She felt it wasn't deserved, that too much damage had been done.

During that last week, she had a sale, opened up the house and let almost all of their things be taken: the couch, her bed, the rocking chair in her daughter's room, the candleholders, the kitchen table, the wall hanging in the living room. She gave a friend her daughter's crib, and what didn't sell, she dropped off at the local thrift store. She left the cleaning supplies under the sink, the Windex, the Comet, even the vacuum cleaner in the utility closet, not knowing that this was the beginning of leaving things behind.

Years from now, the photograph on her refrigerator, the one of the sign that reads *BEGIN*, will be surrounded by appointment reminders, postcards, and her daughter's art.

On the last night in Utah, as the sun shifted behind the trees, she swept the porch for the last time, propped the broom against the corner beside the window, the place where she found it on the day they moved in. The next morning, she pulled out of the driveway hoping that leaving a story meant it would end.

It didn't. She's telling it to you now.

A VERY SHORT ESSAY

The landscape here is light, open, and she thinks that she is, in fact, leaving it all behind, but it's coming with her, even though she has pared down what they own into what will fit into the back of her white Ford Escape. Hours before, she dropped her daughter off at a family's house for two weeks and set down everything she and her daughter owned, except for her black suitcase, in their garage. Driving through the rolling hills of eastern Idaho, she has no idea that the woman she decidedly left in Utah will linger like a character introduced in an early chapter. Turn the page, she's there, portrayed between the pages of recurring themes, unexpected settings.

She takes a left onto Highway 84 and drives fifty-four more miles before pulling into the Motel 6 in Twin Falls. The next morning, she calls her daughter, tells her she's halfway there, and then she heads north on U.S. 75 toward Ketchum, understands why it's called Sun Valley. She passes through Hailey, admires the vertical sign of the Liberty Theater, its outdoor box office window. When she crosses the city limits of Ketchum, she wanders up and down Main Street in search of the cemetery. She stops at a gas station to ask the guy working inside how to get to Hemingway's grave. He can do that, and he will shuffle out into the parking lot, tell her where it is as cars slowly pass and a thin man walks by with his small black dog on a blue leash. The gas station man gives directions and then begins to tell her how Jack came back to Ketchum and drank himself to death, and she'll watch him lower his head when he tells her, "The guy just fell apart." She thinks about how she's trying herself not to become some cautionary tale. He shakes her hand as she thanks him, and he goes back inside the station while she starts up her Escape and takes a left, back the way she came. She finds the small cemetery and drives beneath the arched sign over its entrance toward the set of pine trees in the back. No one else here on a Tuesday afternoon.

She'll stand at the grave, hug her arms against the crisp air, note the pennies scattered on the stone slab. She thinks of the way those two dates tell the introduction, the conclusion, and of all the things between that might be read elsewhere, or not at all. She walks back toward the open door of her car and grabs a penny from the cup holder. Then she sets it on the bottom right corner like the end to a sentence and walks away.

MISSOULA, MONTANA

SUMMER 2006

■

RUNNING AWAY FROM RUNNING AWAY

The Traveler's Inn is a motor lodge on Reserve Street in Missoula, Montana, and the tired lady behind the desk is asking me how long I plan to stay. I tell her a week, maybe more, ask if there's a pool. She asks if I have any pets, tosses her arm back in the direction of the placard (*$10 Deposit for All Pets NO Exceptions*) on the wall behind her. I tell her no, it's just me. Maybe she didn't hear me ask about the pool. She has me fill out an automobile card, and in the space for *make*, I write *Escape*, think how apt the word is now that I've done it. She gives me a key attached to an elongated plastic diamond with the name of the hotel and a number—38. I pull around to the left of the office where she showed me on the hotel map and park in the last space available. Mine is the room on the end and the age I will be in two years. I put my key into the lock and open the door, pull my heavy black suitcase up over the step, and feel for the light switch on the wall, flip it up.

I have come to this city to find an apartment and a job so Indie and I can move here. I cannot know this now, but years later, I'll see this decision to leave academia as some attempt to replay those best days with Kenny when I did this very thing: took off one summer, trading classrooms and office hours for an assigned section and a swinging door to a kitchen. I have come here to write, to wait tables, to wait out a year, perhaps two.

The room is small: one bed, a desk with a mirror, a painting of a lake with snow-capped mountains in the distance, a set of drawers with a TV on it. I grab the remote from the desk and point it at the TV and turn it on, low, because it's late and I don't want to disturb the people who must be sleeping on the other side of the wood-paneled wall. Chris Matthews is leaning over his desk, talking at the camera before cutting to a photo of George W. Bush smiling next to the Japanese prime minister in front of what has to be Graceland. I wonder why Tennessee, why Elvis, why the choice of this place over another, why not a more stately landmark or historical home. I think of the way I chose Missoula over all the other cities, all the other states. I unpack my shorts, my T-shirts, the smaller bag with my toiletries and line them up on the small ledge above the sink in the bathroom. Pulling my swimsuit from the side pocket, I think how I'm always doing things that have nothing to do with what I should be doing. I'm exhausted, from the drive, from the split I've just made of my life. Within minutes, I'm already sleeping to the hum of the air conditioner.

Morning, and I call to check on Indie in Cedar City. I listen to her latest adventures, the trip to the pool they have planned and the banana pancakes they had last night for dinner. When we hang up, I step outside my room to smoke a cigarette and nod at the man who is lugging a duffel and an overstuffed Old Navy bag into his rusted Camry. I have an appointment for nine o'clock at Summit Property Management. I find the building on North Higgins easily, fill out forms, listen to the man who has his glasses low on his nose tell me that there just aren't that many one- or two-bedroom apartments available right now, that he might have something in August, early September. I tell him I need a place in July, and when he looks at my price range, he makes one of those clicking sounds out of the side of his mouth, frowns, tells me I might try Missoula Property Management out on the North Loop.

I'll go there, fill out more forms, get keys to three properties: one, a second-floor apartment with dark wood paneling in the kitchen and a window overlooking a tree with a frayed tire swing; the second, a studio apartment with a butcher block kitchen counter and some bulky, smoke-stained curtains; the third a lower-level apartment I don't even bother going into because the area out front, apparently a shared space with the unit above it, looks like an abandoned yard sale. *Indie*, I think, *would like the tire swing*.

I like being able to go to these places alone, each solitary trip allowing me to pretend I am pulling into the parking lot or parking on the street, coming home. But I don't see myself or Indie in any of these spaces, and I push back the feeling that will get stronger with each apartment I step into, each restaurant manager's hand I shake, each beer I order at the Iron Horse. This will not be our next town; rather, it will not have us.

An afternoon of more keys, more cramped spaces with carpet stains and the pressing smell of kitty litter, of that two-in-the-afternoon emptiness of restaurants, the Uptown Diner, MacKenzie River Pizza Co., The Central Bar & Grill, Catalyst Café, where I squint into the darkness, offer my name but feel like it's not quite mine, listen to women in black slacks and men in short-sleeved shirts gently tell me they're not hiring. One woman walks with me toward the door, telling me she admires what I have done, what I'm doing, trying to live a simpler life. But I don't see it as simple. Even now, I understand how irresponsible I'm being. Indie is four, and the way I see it, this is my last year to be this reckless before she begins school. This year feels like the last one I'll be able to take such a risk, to give up stability for adventure. How can I possibly know that I'll repeat these moves until they dissolve into a pattern? That I will do this again and again and again. How can I know that the risks I take now will progress toward increasingly threatening ones that wait for us in each city, each state, until we almost lose our lives? As I open the door, the woman suggests I try back when the fall semester begins.

Finding a new home, I begin to suspect, requires an allowance, a certain season.

I drive back to my hotel, but not before turning toward the University of Montana campus, where I can see only the tops of buildings through the trees, the Bitterroot Range in the rearview mirror. A university campus seems far away from what I want and who I am right now, especially since I handed in a resignation letter to my department chair at Southern Utah University just three weeks ago.

I feel suspended between two worlds here—the one I left and the one I'm trying for, but all I have so far is the end room of a single-story motel in Missoula, Montana.

Back on Reserve Street, across from the Traveler's Inn, I walk into the Blue Canyon, a mountain-cabin–themed restaurant with oversized booths. I sit down and pull Jo Ann Beard's *The Boys of My Youth* out of my purse and turn to "Out There." I have just read, "I'm running away from running away from home," when the server comes over and takes my order.

I have disappeared here, and I can feel it.

But it's not the good kind of disappearing. It's the kind that evolves when a world won't let me in and I lose who I might have been before, who I'm trying to be in it now.

I wish someone would give me a job and a decent apartment. I wonder how long I can live in Room 38 in a town where I know no one, where no one knows me or anything about what I've left and what I'm left with.

I think how being unknown is its own escape.

The second glass of Pinot Grigio has me wistful, and I stare out the window, notice the pool behind the hotel next door. *I can't even pick the right hotel*, I think, which makes me doubt all my recent decisions. My curly-haired server, I can tell, has been cut from her shift and keeps straightening Sweet'N Low packets in the booths around me, asking if I'd like more water, perhaps a piece of cheesecake. I ask for my check so she can go home, but not before I ask if they're hiring.

I think maybe I shouldn't drink in a restaurant alone in the middle of the day when I've only got two months of money in the bank before my account is depleted. My server tells me it took two months before any place would call her back when she came here three years ago.

I don't have that kind of time. I don't have enough money.

But the desperation of abandoned apartment rooms and empty chairs in downtown restaurants will not be what I remember about this place when I drive south after two weeks of searching, after two weeks of sleeping beneath a scratchy comforter. It will be the man I saw on the corner of Spruce outside the Iron Horse Brew Pub, when I was looking for a place to park.

It's the part of the late afternoon when the sun sets itself down, and the sky is like a pool of water that the sun's descent has disrupted, its myriad of pinks, purples, and oranges released, churning beneath the surface. The corner of Spruce and Higgins is a busy intersection, lots of foot traffic and cyclists, and when I turn right, I catch the watery blue eyes of a gray-bearded man in a red hoodie, a worn backpack slumped beside him. As I pass, he looks right at me, his eyes familiar.

After I find a place on Spruce and park, I cross the intersection I've just driven through, pass the man who's still sitting on the ground, his back against a cement embankment. His eyes smile, and I easily say hello. "Where're you headed?" he asks, as if the two of us had agreed to meet at this hour on this corner years ago.

I point to the doors of the Iron Horse, and he tells me he'll be here when I'm done. Standing next to this bedraggled man feels like a favorite sweater, the navy one I pull out of the closet when it begins to get cold, the one I wear in the house and on trips to the grocery store.

When I come out of the pub, three beers into the evening, he's still on the corner, scanning the intersection, and I offer him a Styrofoam box with half of my cheeseburger in it, cold fries. He accepts it with a direct nod, says he remembers me. But it's not from an hour or so ago that he means.

I accept this, feel not that I remember him, but someone similar, so that being next to him feels like going back to a home I once knew, but lost. Or going back to a home I was too young to know but somehow remember.

At the deli's storefront across the street, a woman in an orange shawl leans against the wall of the building, smoking the stub of a cigarette, her nails yellowed and long. She's wearing snow boots in the summer, the only pair of shoes she owns, I suspect, and I wonder how much it snows here, if the snowfalls last as long as they did in Utah. I think of a night I stood at the front window of that corner house looking out at the canvas of snow, the craggy shadows of the leafless syca-more across the yard in the moonlight.

The grief of losing Kenny buoyed me through the nights, kept me awake, drinking and staring out windows, feeling life to be as empty as those branches casting shadows across the snow. It's a scene that often shows up in my memory, like a photograph in a drawer that shuffles to the top of the pile every time I'm searching for a receipt or a key or an overdue-gas-bill notice.

I cross the street toward the woman, smile at her and the others huddled beside her. I ask her what brand she smokes, and she tells me whatever kind people give her or she finds, but I insist, surely there's one brand she likes more than others. Camels. Inside the deli, I buy myself a pack of Marlboro Lights and her Camels, head over to the cooler and pull out a case of Coors, the man from the corner beside me the whole time. Outside, he introduces me to his community of stained clothes and bent faces, gives the woman my fries. I set the case of Coors on the sidewalk, sit down next to it, tell them all to please, help themselves. They are grateful. While it turns darker, I lean against the bricks of the deli, mostly in silence, a few what-are-you-doing-heres, but mostly my questions, and I know what I have always known, that we all have the same answers: It's not a matter of how, but who. And when. And how often. Or maybe once was enough. Or not nearly enough. And the who, most likely, is us. And so we sit on sidewalks. Or pass people who do.

With the hooded and shawled and shrouded around me, I know that I could go as far into disappearance as it will take me, because I am close to having nothing, and I, too, am without a home. Here I am not a mother, just a woman driving an Escape.

When the case is empty, I stand up, accept the thank-yous and the good lucks, the man's pat on my arm as he warns me that I do not belong here, that this will not be my home, and I realize he knows that better than anyone because he sits on this corner every day watching people, and he read the way I carried myself and what I'm trying to leave behind into and out of the Iron Horse.

Weeks from now, I will drive the extra distance to bring Indie here, to take her to get a burger at the Iron Horse and stay in the Traveler's Inn because I want to show her something, maybe something about myself even though I'd never tell her that this is where I had to go without her to understand, finally, how I was headed in the wrong direction until a good man on a corner patted me on the arm and turned me around.

I reach into the pocket of my blue sweatshirt and pull out the two lottery tickets I bought with the beer. "Here," I tell the gray-bearded man, "I hope you win the world."

I head to my car, hear his voice and turn to see him grinning, his arms stretched out, calling, "I already have!" There's a part of me that wants to stay, not in Missoula, but on this corner, invisible, detached, lost forever, but there's another part of me that knows I need to get back to Indie and avoid this disappearing. The sun is nearly gone, the colors of the sky have settled back to the bottom, and I get into my Escape, unable to look back to something I cannot name.

Two days from now, the woman at the front desk of the Traveler's Inn will call my room to tell me that the entire hotel has been reserved by a group for the next few days, and that I'll need to check out tomorrow by noon. I'll drive to another hotel, one closer to downtown, ten dollars more than Room 38. It will have a pool where I'll swim laps in the mornings to cool down from my three-mile runs before heading out to more properties, more restaurants.

I call the bank to check my account, become nervous. Tomorrow, I will put in an application for the second-story apartment, the one with the tire swing. Fear flashes through my mind like a train passing through the back corners of a small town. It whispers, I'm playing a silly game of "I live in Montana," when what I'm really doing is blowing money and drinking on sidewalks.

Back at my hotel room one night, I sit at the desk built into the dresser against the wall and check my e-mail. There's one from Boise State. Subject: Adjunct Position. The Chair of the Search Committee wants to know if I'm still interested in a position I had forgotten I applied for months ago before I decided where we were headed. It feels like a lifeline, a reaching out across the distance to call me back to what I know and what will put a paycheck in my account in time to avoid the catastrophe of the zero balance that's coming. I add up the numbers, the costs. This e-mail message is a reckoning—I have to do what's best for Indie. I e-mail back, ask for specifics, then I watch *Frasier*, back-to-back episodes, before falling asleep.

The next morning, I check my inbox, find a friendly note from the professor in Boise. He details the position: two classes, no benefits, a list of courses available. I read the list: New Literatures in English, Multicultural Literature, and American Literature II. I would choose two, he writes, start classes on August 16. I hit reply, tell him I'll take the first two on the list, wonder what "New Literatures in English" means. I call Indie, tell her I'm on my way back.

Afternoon, and I pull my black suitcase out of my room, check out of the hotel before heading downtown, where I hope to find the man in the red hoodie, but the corner is quiet, even the front of the deli is empty, so I turn my Escape in the direction of the I-93 South sign, forget that my black swimsuit is hanging over the shower rod in the hotel room, still dripping from the morning's long swim.

BOISE, IDAHO

2006

■

243: The Professor of Longing
Dr. Jill Talbot
Contact: talbot1@boisestate.edu | 426-7060
Office: LA 102 C (a room I share with a broken shelf and three people I never see)
Office Hours: before and after class and once in a booth in the Hyde Park Bar & Grill

Course Description: This course is about failed attempts. It's about me standing in an office two states and two months ago handing over a letter declaring that I was leaving academia indefinitely. It's about being on the road—Utah, Idaho, Montana—climbing north before having to turn around, scramble south. It's about the trying months of summer and ending up in a circumstance not on any map. It's about Boise instead of Missoula, adjustments instead of adventure, impediments edging out impulse, bimonthly paychecks that can't cover rent and daycare, and my last cigarette. It will be writing in a cramped corner on a plastic TV tray in a foldout chair bought at a thrift store. By the end of the semester, the focus will be two AM phone calls and bad checks. For the final, look for a bookcase and a loveseat in a living room with the front door left wide open, Indie's favorite polka-dotted vest forgotten on the loveseat.

Texts: We're not going to read anything beyond my own proclivities. We'll discuss stories, essays, and poems that remind me of my most recent misgivings, the words underlining my past. Our study will include recurring images, my own, of course, as well as the themes of my disposition. The text in this class is me.

Attendance: It's strange to think I'm even here. Years from now, I will feel as if these months were nothing more than an interruption, a curve in the story's road.

Disclaimer: While these aren't the texts I really used that semester, they most accurately reflect who I was during those weeks when I kept my eyes to the sidewalk.

AUGUST 22
Walt Whitman and Emily Dickinson, Selections

Whitman has many famous lines about celebrating himself and containing multitudes and taking to the open road, sounding his barbaric yawp, yet stylistically, he used a device called "cataloging." A long list. Write that down. It's important, because we all catalog, make long lists of lovers, of things to pack, pros and cons, items at the drugstore. Some catalogs come with details, like wine lists. Some come in a shorthand no one but us can read, and if enough time goes by, neither can we, as we pull a forgotten slip of paper from the bottom of a purse or a pocket and stare at a mystery.

Dickinson used dashes in her lines, random capitalization, difficult-to-decipher punctuation. She wasn't consistent in her usage, and often her poems were in unfinished forms. But it's the dashes that draw me, so we'll focus on those. Sometimes they appear at the end of a line, others in the middle, interruptions. Still, other poems are words alone, no dashes at all. Emphasis? A writer's pen carrying over to the next word, down the line? Never intended as part of the prosody at all, like a pause in a conversation misinterpreted as silence or disagreement when it's only a search for the right words? Or are they like bridges crossing a question?

We'll be seeing these elements throughout the semester: catalogs of loss, of what lies between or is left to the end, the choices too difficult to decipher.

Let's start with an opening line of Dickinson's: "You left me, sweet, two legacies—"

It's no surprise that I read Kenny into this line. The legacy of our years together that began with the Eagle River and a half moon. The other, the sweetest legacy, our daughter, who, I suppose, he never saw as part of his prosody. After all, he hasn't seen her since she was six months old. He hasn't expressed a desire to see her. He has never once tried to be a part of her life. That dash—his disappearance. And so, to the Whitmanesque open road he went, "afoot and lighthearted," while, me? My lines are a bit further down: "I carry my old delicious burdens . . . . I carry them with me where I go / I swear it is impossible for me to get rid of them."

The delicious burdens I bear because no state, not this one or the last three I've lived in, can trace a line after Kenny and make him pay child support. He's the dash that keeps dashing, a catalog of unanswered letters.

AUGUST 29

Kate Chopin, "The Story of an Hour"

A "storm of grief" I know well. And that feeling of being locked in a room alone and looking out of it, fearing the feeling that's coming and not being able to beat it back. For years I wanted to be free, and yet, I had "loved him—sometimes." Here is the conflict in—the balance of—maintaining individuality while sharing a life with someone. I'll tell you I've always wanted to share a duplex with a man, him on one side, me on the other, so we have our separate spaces together, but I will not divulge that sharing a life with someone is not a thing I've ever been able to sustain, that I have repeatedly chosen "self-assertion" over "possession," that I can discuss love within the context of a work of literature, but maintaining it, for me, is an "unsolved mystery."

If you need to see me before class, check outside the double doors on the east side of the building. I'll be huddled near a trash can, smoking like a stranger outside a convenience store.

SEPTEMBER 5

Charlotte Perkins Gilman, "The Yellow Wallpaper"

I am trapped inside my own yellow walls. The apartment I rented on Dewey Street, about a ten-minute drive from the University, is the middle unit in a three-unit structure. It is undoubtedly the smallest, crammed between the other two. The landlord who met me at the property in late July on my drive back from Montana opened the door to a hideous site: yellow walls with accents of a deep red, a clash so revolting I almost didn't step inside. Gilman's description resonates:

"The color is repellent, almost revolting; a smoldering unclean yellow." But there were only two weeks before classes began, the other apartments I had seen not livable or in questionable neighborhoods, and I still had to drive back to Utah to pick up Indie.

The apartment has a bathroom off of the kitchen, a proximity that bothers me, a stand-only shower, a tiny bedroom, one closet. This is the smallest place I have ever lived, including the years in graduate school. Indie and I share a bed, one we found in the storage shed out back, and we sit side by side on a loveseat, which barely fits along the wall. The state tells me I make thirty dollars over the limit to qualify for assistance. I think that's about what I spend on smokes a month.

Gilman admitted to altering her experience in her story, using "embellishments and additions, to carry out the ideal." The ideal, she felt, was to keep women from going crazy. Later this semester, while Indie sleeps, I will sit on the loveseat in the middle of the night, cutting my arms with nail scissors, assume this is what is happening to me.

SEPTEMBER 12

Willa Cather, "Paul's Case"

Paul is what is considered a fragmented character. He embodies two worlds but doesn't really live in either. My mother, on voice mail, asks, "Where are you living?" And I'm not really sure. I'm not even sure I'd call what I'm doing here *living*.

Indie's daycare costs $400 a month. Every two weeks, I make just two hundred over that. Then there's the rent, the groceries at Albertson's, the wine I can't stop buying at the state liquor store, not to mention the quarters for pool where

I teach Indie to play while we share a hamburger at the Hyde Park Bar & Grill. I am a fragmented character: I stand before you confident, poised, engaged. I stand inside myself a wreck.

SEPTEMBER 19
Sherwood Anderson, "Mother"

Another window-watching woman. This is a story that uses *where* a character lives as a metaphor for *how* he lives: "The hotel in which he had begun life so hopefully was now a mere ghost of what a hotel should be." I think of my apartment, how it stands for the way there's not enough room here, a suffocation.

SEPTEMBER 26
John Steinbeck, *The Wayward Bus*

I love how the woman in this chapter tells her whiskey glass, "Now you just stay here and wait for me." Alice Chicoy stands inside the screen door of the lunchroom, watching the bus drive away before setting out the *CLOSED* sign and taking a day to herself. In these her hours of rare isolation, she waits on herself, downs a glass of whiskey, then beer, suddenly realizing that "the way you drink changes the taste." At some point, she goes into her bedroom (attached to the diner) and grabs a mirror, sets it down in front of her and serves her selves. I did this last night after I put Indie to bed, sipped Chardonnay in front of the bathroom mirror, keeping myself company. Like Alice, I too have become frightened, worried that I will run out. Of time, of wine, of cities in which to start over.

OCTOBER 3

F. Scott Fitzgerald, "Babylon Revisited"

In the spring semesters, I teach this on or around Indie's birthday. In the fall semesters, I teach it in October, the month five years ago when I wrote to Kenny: "Jack Kerouac wrote that 'everyone goes home in October.' It's October, and the last leaves are falling from the tree outside our bedroom. Come home." Unlike Charlie Wales, he never came back for his little girl. At least Charlie Wales tried.

I love Indie enough for two parents. This part, at least, I get right.

OCTOBER 10

Ernest Hemingway, "A Clean, Well-Lighted Place"

This story is a memory of an afternoon outside our basement apartment in Fort Collins, me in the green chair, Kenny on the porch step, the two of us discussing the old man and the two waiters. During class, I draw the peak of a triangle on the board with a line across the very tip of it, the fractions one-eighth above, seven-eighths below. When I shade in the depths below the surface, I think how the story of us exists so far down that I'm at a level where I can't even see what was there and what never was anymore.

Kenny and I used to smoke on the back porch or balcony of every apartment we shared. Here I smoke on the tiny step outside our apartment. Yesterday, Indie followed me outside and asked me to quit. I said yes. I'm one bad habit down from a pile that's stacked like unwashed dishes in the sink.

OCTOBER 17

John Cheever, "The Swimmer"

This story is about a man who drinks his way home only to find an empty house, all the doors locked. Here we discuss the way a character can look "in at the windows, [see] that the place [is] empty." An inversion of all those other characters who look out, wish to leave.

How can I explain that I'm not even near halfway home, and it's getting darker with every week here, the muddy waters of my life churning, and I'm about to drown?

OCTOBER 24

Tennessee Williams, *A Streetcar Named Desire*

Class cancelled. I just signed a contract for a memoir due in April, and I can't figure out how to start. Anything.

OCTOBER 31

Sherman Alexie, "The Lone Ranger and Tonto Fistfight in Heaven"

I read this last week while sitting at the Hyde Park Bar & Grill in the middle of the afternoon. Alexie writes about anger and imagination being the key to survival, and I can admit, I don't get angry enough, so maybe I balance my survival with what I imagine. I underlined this: "I knew there was plenty of places I wanted to be, but none where I was supposed to be." A recurring theme in literature, the search for a place where one belongs. But it's these questions I'd like to raise, to hear your thoughts: "How do you talk to the real person whose ghost has haunted you? How do you tell the difference between the two?" Because I can't figure that part out.

NOVEMBER 7
Joan Didion, "The White Album"

Didion, similar to Anderson, discusses the house she lived in as being indicative of the times and her own state of mind. Things were fucked up. The world no longer made sense. The center would not hold. "We tell ourselves stories in order to live." I've become very good at this.

Essay Due. Assignment: Discuss the significance of a character's house and his/her relationship to it by focusing on three of the works we have read and discussed. You are also required to discuss two texts (poems, essays, films, stories, novels) that do not appear on this syllabus.

The check I wrote last week at the Hyde Park Bar & Grill bounced. I knew it would.

NOVEMBER 14
Raymond Carver, "The Ashtray" | "Why Don't You Dance?"

A stanza from the poem:

> Then walks back to the table and sits
> down with a sigh. He drops the match in the ashtray.
> She reaches for his hand, and he lets her
> take it. Why not? Where's the harm?
> Let her. His mind's made up. She covers his
> fingers with kisses, tears fall on to his wrist.

A line from the story:

"His side, her side."

Class adjourned.

NOVEMBER 21
Amy Hempel, "Memoir"

An interesting story with only one sentence—enough to tell the story of a life. The three hours of class not enough to explain what that means. I'm unraveling. Can you tell?

NOVEMBER 28
Pam Houston, "Cowboys are My Weakness"

Discussion: "This is not my happy ending. This is not my story."

While you discuss, I've got to go in the hallway to return a phone call from a friend who has called to respond to the frantic message I left on her voice mail at two o'clock in the morning. I'm going to tell her I'm fine, that I'm discussing a story with an unnamed narrator. It won't be a lie.

DECEMBER 5
Tim O'Brien, "The Things They Carried"

We will close our study by examining the effect of Whitman-esque cataloging in prose form and how Lt. Jimmy Cross carries the letters of a girl that he hopes loves him, even though the narrator shows us it isn't so. The young lieutenant reads her words again and again, as if he can change their meaning. When her words distract him from the war, he burns them. Let me clarify: it doesn't matter. He'll read those letters for the rest of his life.

Those misinterpreted letters like the checks I keep writing, and for some reason, I pretend it doesn't matter. My balance already overdrawn past anything I can catch up with in time for the check to clear. Two years from now, I'll send $160 a month to pay down the damage I'm doing here, but for now, I'll keep writing false words and fake numbers on a small slip of paper, convincing everyone but myself they mean anything.

We'll cut the last meeting short, because last night turned into an Alice Chicoy afternoon when I decided there was no way I could stretch my severe salary across another semester, so I've been cataloging my choices for the next city and am in a bit of a panic.

Final: Your final is a representation of what you have learned in this class that may not be measured by exam or essay. I'm bringing a stack of university parking tickets I have accrued over the course of the semester, the manifestation of the fines owed to me, the fines I own.

AN ITINERANT YEAR
{ Part 2 }

SPRING 2007

∎

THE SAGE COUCH

A friend once told her, "When you live in someone else's house, you're one word away from being asked to leave." After only one semester in Boise, she crumbled under the pressure of her adjunct salary, and when she received an advance for her book, it only took a week before it was gone after a pile of bills and overdue rent. Then the state told her she didn't qualify for assistance, and that's when she started scrambling for a way out, a way away. When Anna called and said, "You can live here," she backed up her Escape to the front door of the one-bedroom apartment, loaded it with what she could not do without, what her daughter had asked to take. She left the black bookcase and the loveseat in the living room, the mattress and her Mac Classic II in the storage shed. Of all the things she has left behind, this is one that lingers. She left behind her words—the essays, the poems, the dissertation—all saved on that computer, all locked in a storage shed on a back shelf. She thinks about someone finding it, pulling it down from the shelf and turning it on, clicking through the documents of her twenties to read the roads she was writing, to navigate her wrong turns.

She left the front door open as she burdened the Escape with suitcases and boxes, stacks of clothes on hangers, her daughter's stuffed animals. Beneath it all, the vintage trunk, the one she bought at a flea market ten years before, the one she always uses as a coffee table. The inside of the trunk musty, stained, and she always imagines some traveler in a hat getting caught on a platform in a sudden downpour. She pictures this traveler carrying the trunk on trains, its size cumbersome, the lock on the right side not yet broken, the way it is now.

In Utah, she knew a woman who kept a green suitcase by her front door, a sustained act of almost leaving. This past year, she has carried her suitcases in and out of too many doors, repeated acts of almost staying.

She had lived with Anna and Jack before in Minturn, during the years when they were all younger, more free, before any of them knew that the lives they were waiting to live were never going to rescue them from the ones they were living. Anna and Jack had a sage couch, where she'd nap in the afternoons after working the breakfast shift at the restaurant or sit with Jack's friend when he got off work at the construction site, the two of them telling each other their stories. When she looks back now, she sees how they created a shared narrative based upon the collection of those stories, the very ones they came to know as made up, embellished, or the most disturbing ones, the stories they never told.

Years later, after Jack's friend left her and her daughter, Anna and Jack took them into their house in a small town outside of Boulder. They cleared out an upstairs office so she could have a place for her daughter's crib, changing table, the rocking chair where she read to her every night, where she sang to her before dragging her shuddering heart down to the basement to sleep on a futon to the rushing of the washing machine, the whine of the dryer. He would show up sometimes as if nothing ever happened, as if this was a summer from years ago in Minturn. These were the months of temporary custody, when the court granted him eight hours on Saturdays and four hours each Wednesday, hours she'd long for her daughter feeling as if something within her had disappeared until she could hold her again.

Usually, they'd meet halfway between where she lived in a basement and where he lived in a cabin at the foothills in Boulder—when she'd carefully move their daughter in her car seat from her backseat to the passenger side of his truck. On those afternoons and evenings, when he'd bring their tiny girl back, he'd duck into her car for a few minutes and admit he'd messed everything up. All he needed, he'd say, holding both of her hands, was some more time. Men who leave, she would come to understand, always want out clean, and when they don't get that, they sing a refrain of suffering loud enough to silence the chords of despair they know they've built in another.

In those moments, she'd look at the three of them huddled in the car—feeling the heat from the vents and hearing the *shush* of the wipers sweeping the snow—the two of them in the front, their daughter in the backseat, usually asleep, and she'd convince herself that this is what it would be like, eventually, as long as she was patient, as long as she did nothing to disrupt this fragile balance. After all, most of those nights after they took off for their own roads, they'd talk on the phone until both of them pulled into their separate drives. But it was the times he'd show up that unsettled her, the times he'd call to say he was on his way, the hours, she sees now, that always fell long after her daughter had fallen asleep. He'd make love to her, even stay the night before climbing the basement steps and quietly closing the front door before getting into his blue truck and driving away before dawn. Such duplicity. These were the months she'd find the stack of dishes that Anna and Jack accumulated in the sink. They built a fragile architecture, and she feared that if she were to disrupt their balance, something in her would rupture. She spent her days driving to Boulder and back to finish her degree, all the while checking messages and the curb out front for his truck.

Once, he invited her to stay the night at his cabin. She couldn't help but read his offer as a message: He had finally had enough time. He had finally broken it off with the receptionist. He had chosen her; he had chosen his daughter. How relieved she felt.

That night, she settled their daughter in the playpen he had bought for her. And it was then she began to look around. She walked into his bedroom and noticed the nightstands, one on each side, and then she saw the water bottles, one on his side, one on the other. She understood immediately he did not live here alone. She felt as if she had walked into a scene arranged for someone else, felt the presence of a stranger and knew it was the role she had been cast to play. She moved, determined, to the kitchen, and just as he asked what she was looking for, she flipped on the light to measure the continued pattern, the two wineglasses on a shelf above the sink, the two coffee cups on the counter. How foolish she felt.

She left abruptly, clicking her sleeping daughter into the car seat and driving them through the dark and back to their borrowed rooms. Once in the house, she carried her daughter upstairs to her crib, then stepped out into the hallway and only got as far as the top step before she surrendered to it. Staring into the dark of the living room below, she could see the sage couch, the same one where the two of them had first shared their stories, and she knew she needed to move from here if she were to ever complete the separation. She would stand it for two more months before graduating and getting a teaching position in Utah. Once again, she loaded the Escape and buckled her daughter into her car seat before pulling away as Anna and Jack stood in the driveway, smiling and waving and wishing them well.

Four years pass, and the sage couch shows up like a recurring image, a symbol in a story. This time, the couch sits in a living room in a corner house in a city, in a state none of them has ever been. This time, Anna and Jack do not clear out a room or offer a spacious basement. Instead, they greet her with one room she and her daughter can share. A room with the same futon and a built-in desk, where she will spend most of her time finishing her book, writing about him.

In this, the third house they have shared, they are all disheveled, as if they've gone through unexpected rapids and are still catching their breaths, pretending they're not being pushed along by a current after misreading the water. Anna and Jack are now heavy with the weight of perfunctory careers and paying back student loans. And in the years between, there was the affair, and even though it ended, the mistrust between them smolders. She steps around their tension, sits at their table during mealtime, follows the schedule of their lives, feeling as if she left hers miles away. The two of them still leave stacks of dishes in the sink, and each morning, after Jack has left for the restaurant and Anna has gone to teach her painting class, she carefully pulls each plate, each bowl from the sink and washes it, rinses it, then sets them all in order on the dish rack to dry before she sits down to write while her daughter watches *Ice Age* again or draws pictures at the kitchen table.

No fragile architecture or gentle empathy, this house heavy in a tempest of strained conversations and phone calls taken in another room. What they let pile up—the dishes, the secrets—threatens to crash down with every utterance. Only her daughter roams unabashedly amidst the clutter of this captivity. She has just turned five, so she is too young to know the history, the houses that came before, the narrative that ties them all together.

There is not nearly enough room for three people who would prefer to live out their secrets in private: the role-playing game that keeps Jack locked up in the back room for seven-, eight-hour stints; Anna's former lover in the living room as if he's a student dropping by to pick up some brushes and not the man who wrinkled the canvas. Then there's her. The bottle of Chardonnay in the refrigerator always on display, the way she pours more than she should. Each of them knows they cannot hide here, and in the end, they shudder against the way their secrets look like a mirror floating in front of them as they shuffle in and out of the kitchen. They resent each other, all of it, the years between them, the man who walked away to leave them all feeling responsible, for what, they can't, or won't, say.

She is two chapters away from finishing the book about him. She uses his real name as a matter of record and a way to return his betrayal. It will be years before she realizes that the man she writes is not the man she missed, even more years before she understands she's never been the woman on the page.

Writing the fiction of her past, she does not see how Anna and Jack might misinterpret the story. The tempest in the house now churns to emergency-siren levels. One day, they sit her down on that same sage couch and ask her to move out. She wonders how she got here: to this city, to this couch, to leaving. Again.

Beyond the chance to save money on rent and bills, she wonders why she'd drive halfway across the country to live with them again. But desperation doesn't ask for explanation—it avoids it. And such desperation has ushered her to the wrong places, the wrong decisions, and most of all, toward the wrong version of herself. Every time.

The three of them sit in silence, and she looks at the television in the corner—his television, the one he left behind all those years ago on a day he was too ashamed to ask for anything back from anyone. She sees it now: the ghost she keeps getting on roads to get away from in the reflection of a turned-off television.

Her grief too fragile, too piled up like so many dishes. A viciousness.

She will think of her friend's words, the ones about being one word away. There will be a comment made about the wine, but she suspects it is not the reason for her sudden eviction. It's the stories she has come to know too well, the ones they'd rather not have told, and every time she sits down to write at the desk in that room, they hover, lean into the frame of the open door, terrified that the story she is writing is theirs.

After hearing from a friend about a visiting position at the university where he teaches in Oklahoma, she packs up the Escape for the fourth time this year. She repacks the vintage trunk, the suitcases, and the boxes in back. Her daughter sits in the passenger seat. This time, no one watches them go.

STILLWATER, OKLAHOMA

2007–2011

■

WATCHING OVER NOTHING

At the Chili's on Hall of Fame Avenue, the weekday bartender asks Jeremy, a regular, if he has had anything to eat
just as I sit down at the next stool and open up a copy of *The
Great Gatsby*. I am looking for lines spoken by Daisy, when
she asks what they're going to do today and the day after that.
I talked about the lines in my nonfiction writing class a few
hours ago, when I urged students to step away from the story
and interject a statement, a philosophical pondering. "Open
it up. Develop it," I'd suggested. "Make it mean something
beyond what happened."

Fitzgerald was always doing this—dragging his readers into
"the dark night of the soul," where it is "always three o'clock in
the morning." I asked my students what he may have meant by
this three-o'clock-in-the-morning business. "Maybe," a ball-
capped boy joked, "he meant waiting in Whataburger drive-
thru lines." "Sleeping," said the girl next to him. I stayed quiet,
waiting for a Fitzgerald-worthy answer. A young man confessed to a recent night of walking the streets at that very hour.
Another remembered that Fitzgerald himself was a drunk and

guessed it might have been his "coming around" hour. I liked that one. A couple of students mentioned insomnia. "Yes," I said, adding, "Hemingway ends a 'A Clean, Well-Lighted Place': 'After all, many must have it.'" A few students wanted to know what "it" was—so I did what I always do and asked what they thought, but they pressed back. They wanted to know if I knew. I said, "Indeed," and I shifted the conversation back to making meaning.

I flip through the novel's pages, looking for the blue of my underlines. Always blue.

Today is a Pinot Noir afternoon for me, and it is my last time in this bar, but I do not know it. Jeremy and the bartender, Angela, start laughing about the latest episode of *The Office* while I find Nick Carraway at the end of another chapter, "watching over nothing." Jeremy stands and pays carefully for his beers before nodding to me on his way out. Once he's outside, I point to his empty stool and ask Angela, "What's his story?"

"He's a meth addict."

I feel guilty for asking. This is too private. I shift in my seat, look around.

Dary, a big-haired woman always in dark florals, plops down two stools away and orders her usual, the Gran Patrón margarita, a dangerous drink served in an oversized blue martini glass. She'll knock back two of those swimming-pool-size cocktails before foisting herself off the stool on her way back to work, where she clicks a button to send my paycheck via direct deposit from Oklahoma State University every two weeks. I order my second Pinot, see a heavyset man in flannel and crease-in-the-front jeans amble into the bar area. He barks two words, "Bud. Tall," before Angela can place a coaster in front of him. The Bud Tall guy wants to know what everyone does for a living. He's breaking protocol as all of us sit, staring ahead in our own private Oklahomas. Angela winks at me and then tells him I'm a writer.

"Yeah? Hey, that's really cool. Did you write that?" He points to *Gatsby*.

I am polite, say no, and understand that the world I live in has no meaning for him whatsoever.

A quiet man sits across the bar over a glass of Pinot Grigio, and I am reminded of the last time I was here, when I spent an afternoon with Grigio and Didion. A few paragraphs, a few sips, and on it went like that until I was at the bottom of my second glass, and every line I read was blue-underline poignant. That's when I know it's time to go. Strange, how we create ways to measure our limits or convince ourselves we adhere to them.

The Pinot Grigio man's name is Peter. He recently broke up with his lover, who argues he drinks too much. "But," Peter perks up, "we manage our vulnerabilities." I grab a napkin and write that down with my blue pen. When I get home, I'll place the napkin on my writing desk—where it stays as a reminder.

I go back to reading. "What'll we do with ourselves this afternoon," cried Daisy, "and the day after that, and the next thirty years?" *Not this*, I think. With the restaurant empty except for those of us in the bar, I ask for my check, tip Angela heartily, and leave the end of my Pinot in the glass.

RADIO SILENCE

I am driving west on Highway 51. It's Tuesday, the day before Indie's ninth birthday, and as I pass the city limits of Stillwater on my way to Oklahoma City, I switch from the Sinatra station, the one playing "I'll Be Seeing You," to the '70s station, the one playing The Marshall Tucker Band's "Heard It in a Love Song." *I'm gonna be leavin' at the break of dawn.* I rarely listen to the song now, though sometimes when Indie is in the car, I'll let it play, even sing along, assume the next time she asks me why her father left, I can say, "You know that song, the one about the guy who never had a damn thing but what he had, he had to leave it behind?" She'll know the song. So many times, when she's singing along to Ambrosia or Bread, Jackson Browne, especially America, in the car, I ask her how she knows all the words to those long-ago songs, and she always has the same answer, "You sing all the time."

Kenny used to tell me that, too.

I change the station to NPR.

I recognize a familiar voice:

> *The American family has changed. The nuclear family in the house across the street is still there, but different kinds of families live on the block, too: unmarried parents, gay parents, people who choose not to have children at all, and, of course, single parents.*
>
> *A new Pew Research poll asked Americans about these trends and found almost 70 percent believe that single women raising children on their own is bad for society.*
>
> *Of course, there is a wide array of single mothers. Some women choose to raise children by themselves. Others find themselves without a partner through divorce or abandonment. But when seven in ten believe this is bad for society, it makes you wonder.*
>
> *So we want to hear from single mothers today. How do people treat you? Tell us your story. 800-989-8255 is the phone number. E-mail us, talk@npr.org. You can also join the conversation on our website. Go to npr.org. Click on TALK OF THE NATION.*

I grip the steering wheel and glance at my cell phone in the cup holder. I keep my eyes out for a rest stop.

Abandonment: If there's a box that single mothers check to identify their status, that's the one I'd check, but Neal Conan's mention of it is the first time I've ever heard it publicly acknowledged. I settle into my seat, take a sip of my latte, and turn up the volume. I am making the curve near the trees, so I am close to the I-35 junction.

All the single mothers I have known have been single in self only, but not in parenthood—there are weekends, summer weeks, joint custody. Even I have documents that refer to me, the custodial parent, and Kenny, the non-custodial one, documents with our names, hers, and our Social Security numbers. Such distancing rhetoric.

I wonder if the rest stops in this area have cellular service. In north central Oklahoma, phone calls often drop behind the barren, intermittently burned landscape.

When Indie turned two, I went to my third-floor office at school and found a box leaning against my locked door. Kenny had sent her a book and a letter. It remains the only contact he has ever made with her, the only thing he has ever given her, and she was too young to know it. I keep them in a box for her, along with the dress she was wearing the last time he saw her, a plaid, quilt-patterned sundress, size: six months. Thinking of it now, I realize how small she was when he walked away.

————————

When Indie asks why he left, it feels the way Hemingway described good writing, that the seven-eighths beneath the surface is what truly moves the narrative. But I am always honest, yet fair—recalling the counseling the State of Colorado required—a parent should never speak in negative terms of the other parent. The child bases her identity on who she comes from, so belittling or demeaning the other parent belittles the child.

Last year, Indie suffered from recurring dreams of a robber coming into the house and leaving. After I asked a few questions, I got up the nerve to ask her, "Indie, do you think the man might be your father?" She said yes. The robber, the unknown man who kept showing up unexpectedly, the one who kept leaving, was him, and what he kept stealing was a part of her life. I told her I used to dream of him standing outside the front lawn of our house. She said she dreams of men outside the house, too.

———————

Conan is pointing out the fact that our president was raised by a single mother. His guest, a Pew Center senior researcher, Mr. Moran, responds:

> *Exactly right. It doesn't mean you can't grow up to be president. It just means that the chances . . . the likelihood that bad things will happen is increased if you grow up in a single-parent household.*
>
> *Did the same results obtain if you said: What if they're raised by a single father?*
>
> *Interesting. We did not ask . . . we didn't ask that. Since most single-parent households are by women, it's . . . the real issue is single moms.*

The real issue is in the survey, the glaring omission that mirrors the very men who leave, who refuse responsibility for their children. Whether the reason is addiction, those men whose relationship with booze or drugs is more important than any they might have with their children; those men who get a whole new family, or choose a new love, or the one that applies to Kenny, the "grass-is-greener-on-the-other-side-of-that-hill,"

Marshall Tucker Band mentality. The real issue is men who leave whatever they have for whatever they want. The men who shrug off responsibility like a truckload that slows them down.

Once, not long before he left, Kenny took off for a night out, and I chased him down the three flights of stairs and out to the parking lot. Panting, I ran alongside his truck with my hands gripping the window ledge of his door and asked, "Where are you going?" He stopped and shifted to park. He wouldn't look at me. He looked out his windshield as if to a place as far away from me and Indie as he could see.

"I'm trying to find a life," he mumbled.

"I thought we had a life."

I knew it was only a matter of time.

Some fathers leave. There's nothing to be done about it. The worst is when I'm asked to explain it—to strangers, to friends or family, to Indie.

According to the U.S. Census Bureau, 7 percent of ten million custodial mothers do not receive child support. That's one in fourteen. I am one of them.

Nineteen percent with bachelor's degrees or more do not receive support. Only 26.9 percent have at least an associate's. I have a PhD.

Thirty-four percent have never been married. That's me.

Twenty-five percent are forty and over. Check.

A man named Alan from Fulton, New York, has called into the show. His voice is sincere.

> ALAN: *Well, single fathers run into some of the same things that I've been hearing on the show, that, you know, just the way that you can actually do that by yourself, you know, without a woman around, in your case with a single mom, without a man around and so forth.*
>
> CONAN: *But did you feel the stigma?*
>
> ALAN: *More disbelief, I think, or wonder, you know.*

Rosalind, Zelda Fitzgerald's sister, did not think her brother-in-law, Scott, could raise his daughter, Scottie, on his own after Zelda was institutionalized for a nervous breakdown.

Scottie grew up to claim that had her father not been her father, she could have been an extraordinary woman. More times than not, I am glad the man who left us is not a part-time father, and I understand how much more complete Indie would feel if she knew him, how she "beat[s] on, boat against the current, borne back ceaselessly into the past" because a large part of her past disappeared before she even began, and there's no green light at the end of a dock for her to gaze upon, there's just the gaping distance between her and what she might hope to regain, though it never should have been hers to lose.

Shelly from Chapel Hill is the next caller. She is not a single mother, but she works with juvenile kids accused of crimes.

Here come the statistics, I think, the ones about children raised without a father, the 80 percent increase in drug use and dropout rate. I think of turning back to the radio, something a bit more soothing for my drive, like Sinatra, or maybe something upbeat, the '80s station. Shelly continues:

> *When I—you know, when I heard the Pew Institute study that single motherhood is bad for society, I found that statement really problematic as though it's the mother's fault.*
>
> *You know, I think the system, our laws, our schools, our judges, are prejudiced against single mothers.*

Even though I knew Kenny would have nothing to do with Indie, my lawyer insisted we go to court, warned that the law had grown exceedingly sympathetic to fathers to ensure their rights and that there was little chance he would simply vanish. "Listen to me," I told her as I leaned across her desk, "he already has. He's gone." Yet Kenny was the one who insisted we establish custody, another unknown coordinate of our complicated history, and it was I, during the months leading up to the hearing, who lived in fear that he might get Indie. For one, I had a lawyer spouting off case after case of a legal system showing preference to fathers. Two, I was in the process of completing an MFA, no stronghold when it comes to procuring employment. Finally, I had his words in my head from nights I'd sit on the back porch with a glass of Chardonnay, listening to his voice on the phone that it was I, not him, who wanders, who moves from place to place and never settles.

Those words come back to me when Indie can name all the states she has lived in: Colorado, Utah, Idaho, Kansas, Oklahoma. We've lived in Oklahoma the longest, four years, and my restlessness and desire to pack up and move on again is balanced only by my accountability to her via income and health insurance. Might the fellows at the Pew Research Center, and their respondents, consider responsibility in their survey? Surely the Boulder County Court did not take into consideration that morning in June who had left whom, who was already living a new life across town. I was told by the judge to find a job before the June 23 hearing, and that if she chose, she could limit my job search to Colorado because the best scenario for Indie would be to have her mother and father together in the same town. The judge reminded me that she would have to approve any out-of-state job I was offered. No one, not the judge, not my lawyer, would listen to me when I repeated that proximity was not the issue, that the whole hearing was a nonissue, that he would play father in court and then walk out and disappear.

———

The other day, Indie and I were at the university library circulation desk, where I was checking on a missing book. She picked up a stamper. I'd noticed it before, a stamp with a word on it to signify a book's status in the system. She asked what it was for, and I shrugged. While I wasn't looking, she stamped the inside of her left hand. She held it up to me, the red ink on her palm: ABANDONED.

Jack Kerouac refused to acknowledge his own daughter, Jan, claiming, "She's not my daughter," then going to great lengths to avoid child support by maintaining that he was abroad. The letters he wrote to Jan's mother in 1956 were mailed to Allen Ginsberg, who could send them to her with a Casablanca postmark so that Kerouac would appear out of the country. When Jan was only four, Kerouac showed a snapshot of a beautiful, dark-haired child on a tricycle to his then-girlfriend, writer Joyce Johnson, who described in her epistolary memoir, "anyone could see that little Jan's resemblance to him was unmistakable, and I told him so." Johnson notes that Kerouac "refused the role of father" and that his greatest fear was "losing the freedom that enabled him to write."

Jan only met her father twice: once when she was nine, when Kerouac finally agreed to take a blood test, which proved his obligation to pay child support, and again at fifteen, when she paid him a visit. A biography, *Use My Name: Jack Kerouac's Forgotten Families*, refers to Kerouac's detached comment to Jan during that unfocused meeting, telling her that she could "use his name." Jan described that last visit in an interview, her father's refusal to move from the recliner in his mother's living room, where he was drinking whiskey and watching *The Beverly Hillbillies*.

Jan lived a troubled life, including some time working as a prostitute in New Mexico. Having published two novels, both autobiographical and both revealing a penchant for the road, just like her father, she died from kidney failure at the age of forty-four.

I pick up my phone when I hear Conan begin to recite the 800 number again. A woman named Paige is talking about sociology:

> *I do think that sociologically, it does have a lot to do with our culture and the way that our culture views women. I think that it's telling that the question didn't get asked of men raising children by themselves. And I think that part of the negative view of women raising children on their own is because of the view that our culture has of women.*

Conan clarifies, *Is this about sexism?* Answer from the Pew researcher: *Well, we don't want to demonize single mothers.*

I put the phone down, traffic has picked up, and I turn my blinker on to merge right and avoid the overbearing pickup behind me, thinking about how people treat me. While there are exceptions, the most common response is "I don't know how you do it. I know I couldn't do it." But how do you know what you can do unless you're not given a choice? Other common responses include faces full of either pity or questions. I recall an elderly woman from down the street in Utah who drove up in her white Buick just days after Indie and I had moved into our house to yell out, "I hear you're a single mother!" as a greeting. I think of Indie's teachers, the ones who flash that wincing smile during parent-and-teacher conferences or blatantly assume I am the deadbeat. "Um, do you work, Miss . . . um, what would you like for me to call you?" I am the sole caretaker.

I am the sole caregiver. My background in literary theory informs me that I am Other.

———————

I take the exit for I-35 South, trying not to get dizzy as I make the full-circle ramp to the highway, always sure this will be the time when I will miss the gaps in semi-traffic and be forced to the shoulder, both me and the car shuddering. After an e-mail from someone named Shelly in Durham, North Carolina, who claims to have taken the survey and answered "bad for society" based upon economic hardship and our society's refusal to help, Conan announces another guest:

> *Mary Pols, a journalist who reviews books and movies for* Time *magazine, also a single mother. Her memoir is titled* Accidentally On Purpose: The True Tale of a Happy Single Mother, *and she joins us today from Maine Public Broadcasting Network in Portland, Maine. Nice to have you with us today.*

A journalist for Time, I think, *probably not a single mother who suffers economic hardship*, as I slow to seventy-eight when I notice an Oklahoma State Patrol car in my rearview mirror. The officer passes, and I resume at eighty, sure that one speeding fine would not upend the monthly budget of Ms. Pols, who has just commented that her economic status improved once she became a single mother because she was motivated to provide for her son, an incentive that caused her to work harder professionally than she ever had before.

We moved from Utah because I wanted to provide a more diverse and bohemian experience for Indie as she was nearing the age of five and soon would be entering kindergarten and developing a personality I can only describe as her inner-hippie. My initial plan was to take out some retirement money and live in Missoula, where I could wait tables and have the rest of the time to write, but true to the pockets of the West, Missoula was not welcoming to outsiders. So when Boise State offered me an adjunct position that offered no health insurance and $1220 a month in my bank account, I immediately accepted it. And even though Indie and I loved BSU's campus, the Smokey Mountain Pizzeria, the bright blue field of Bronco Stadium, and the burger joint in Hyde Park where I taught her to play pool, and even though I ran behind as she wobbled on her bike with training wheels up and down the trail along the greenbelt, it was not enough.

I stood in line at the state assistance office for two hours and filled out all the required paperwork, then went home and waited for the assistance I was sure would come. Two weeks went by before I received a letter from the state regretting to inform me that I made too much money to qualify. With the letter still in hand, I called their offices to learn that they judged on gross, not net, and that my salary, as it were, the one that paid me for teaching three classes, and the one that was supposed to cover over $400 in daycare and food and $350 in rent (we lived in a one-bedroom apartment) was thirty dollars beyond the state limit. This after both Utah and Idaho child support agencies had assured me that they had contacted Colorado and were working on my file.

Boulder County told Kenny that June morning to pay $634 per month, and before we adjourned, he stood and asked to make a plea to the judge. I remember bracing myself, wondering if the bare minimum wasn't what he wanted after all. But no, he coldly stated, "I don't think I should have to pay because I'm not going to see her." It turns out this is the way he worked out the math: no presence, no payment. Rework the equation; it's not equivalent.

The Pew researcher notes, in an unsympathetic tone, that it's the children who pay the price. I nod, sip the last of the now-cold latte, taste the nutmeg particles that have settled at the bottom. He's right. Indie is asked repeatedly by other children, "Where's your dad?"

"What do you tell them?"

"That he left."

The Pew researcher, apparently, has left the show, but not before citing some study that the level of a parent's education makes no difference. I suppose this means that my four degrees offer no brace against the statistics.

Neal Conan has asked Mary Pols to make some final comments. It seems I have missed my chance to speak as an abandoned single mother, but Pols is offering a unique story of her own, though I can't help but scoff at the subtitle of her memoir, *The True Tale of a Happy Single Mother*. Apparently, in Pols's case, a girl walks into a bar, meets a guy, gets pregnant, and chooses to raise the child on her own. An "accidentally, on purpose" adventure of going it alone. I admire that. The Roz Doyle approach to single mothers. But wait, she's saying something else:

> *You know, my son's father is, you know, he's in California. We're in Maine now. But he has been an active part in my son's life.*
>
> *And, you know, every school that my child has been at has had both of our phone numbers.*

If you have the address and phone number of the father of your child and he's an "active part of your son's life," you are in no way close to the level of single mother that I am. Single as in only. Single as in one. Not one at this house plus one at that house, which equals two. I'm saying that in my life, the father is not an option on the school's who-can-pick-up list.

———

I was in the wood aisle of Lowe's a few weeks before last Christmas. Indie had asked Santa for wood, hammer, and nails so that she could "build things." After roaming around the aisle looking at various widths and lengths of wood, I decided to forgo my I-can-figure-this-out facade and went over to the large woodcutting machine, where I saw a guy with one of those aprons and a Lowe's nametag. I told him what I needed, different sizes of boards, of wood, because my eight-year-old daughter had asked Santa for wood so that she could build things.

The man looked at me, askance, stared at the boards already in my basket, while I felt tiny and ridiculous in the oversized store—the sheer height of their aisles is enough to intimidate those like me who have no idea what most of the stuff in the store is for; though for people like Kenny, the kind of guy who took a tool belt to work, it's a paradise, which is why I look around at floor-covering samples and storm doors and think, "If only you were here." The bearded man erupts with a "what a unique child" then wants to know what Indie wants to build and if she might want a subscription to *Woodworking Magazine.* He disappears behind one of the large aisles and comes back, flipping through an issue. He seems lost in his own love of woodwork, as if he is imagining the possibilities of what she might build, the way I'm sure Kenny would, the way I saw him do so many times, measuring, configuring, planning. Since Indie has been able, she has taken things apart to see how they are put together—clocks, game systems, lamps. She tells me she likes to see how things work, and she likes to disassemble pieces and put them together again. Words Kenny always said as he went through the same take-apart, put-back-together process. When he left, he disassembled me.

I ask the man if he has children, and he tells me he has a daughter, nine, and I ask him what she has asked for from Santa. "I have no idea," he tells me, "she lives with her mother in Tulsa, and I never see her, but I can tell you, she's nothing like your daughter." And then I get uncomfortable, wonder what this man has done to exclude himself from his daughter's life and feel more empathy for his daughter than sympathy, which he clearly does not require, as his flippancy about his own child irks me.

Years after Frank Sinatra left his wife and three young children for Ava Gardner, he would tell his youngest, Tina, "I was selfish—my choices would affect you forever."

Since I started listening to this program, I have intermittently shouted across the interior of my car and through the windshield to the highway before me, to the leafless trees, their branches craggy and sharp, to the overcast sky: "Why isn't anyone talking about the absent fathers?" And then Mary Pols says this:

> It's funny—if the survey had said, for instance, instead of, you know, do you think that single mothers raising children without fathers or without male figures are bad for society? What if it had said, you know, are absentee fathers good for society or bad for society?

Finally. But the question is never answered, and Mr. Conan tosses to a break. I exit to Second Street outside of Oklahoma City, fifty-four miles from where I began, and where I come every other Tuesday or Thursday. Sometimes, I drive here and turn around, sometimes I eat lunch at On the Border, sometimes I wander one of the Oklahoma City Malls for an hour or so, and on occasion, I bring my running shoes and explore unfamiliar streets before I have to get back to pick up Indie from school.

———————

At the intersection, I press the first button preset, the '70s station. America. "Sister Golden Hair." Indie really likes this one. I sing along.

SINGLE MOTHER

This morning, I stood out in the yard, the lingering green of the grass peeking through leaves heavy with yesterday's rain. I tossed a slobbery ball, again and again, for Blue, our heeler/boxer mix, as she chased it down in the liminal moment of pre-sunrise, the light slicing the slats in the back fence. When I turned to throw the ball in the other direction, I found the moon, sheer white in the darkness of the west. I reveled in the betweenness of it all: night and day, sunrise and moonset, the way Blue never drops the ball at my feet, the way she nearly returns but never comes back all the way. It makes me wonder where the line is between preference and stubbornness. Kenny's like that. I don't know where he is, but every day, he comes back in Indie's dimples or the shape of her legs, the curve of her upper teeth, the way she holds her mouth the exact same way he did during sleep, or the look she gives me when she's not quite sure I know exactly what she has done that she's not supposed to do. In those moments, Kenny comes back, but not all the way.

It is 3:12 AM on a Saturday in February, a snowstorm drapes the windows, and the Rolling Stones are playing a song, though I can't remember which one. I had asked for Sinatra, but they said they didn't have any in the OR, so I settled for a classic rock station. I wish I could remember the song, and I wish I could ask Kenny if he remembers, but even before she was born, he began making small departures: a suspicious errand during my thirty-three hours of labor that emptied our bank account of all but four dollars; the days after in the hospital room when he went back to work even after his boss told him to stay with me and Indie. In those long, empty afternoons, I checked out film after film from the volunteer who came by with a cart of DVDs. I saw *Sunset Boulevard* for the first time there, though I remember little of it.

Back home with Indie, we sat far apart on the futon, Kenny's attention toward *Junk Yard Wars*. I'd ask him to take a turn to change her or to check on the noises we could hear her make from her yellow room—the one he painted, the one he bordered with pastel giraffes and elephants and dancing hippos, the border he took a piece of and affixed to the light switch as a final touch—but he'd refuse to even turn from the television and mutter, "I don't want to get too attached in case I leave." And then came the morning when he finally allowed himself to do just that.

When I wined my way into rehab a year or so after Kenny left us, my counselor asked me during one of our weekly sessions for an example of the ways in which my relationship with wine had taken over my life, or as they always put it in rehab: "How has your drug of choice caused you to leave your own life?"

I tell him this story: It is the season of fallen leaves, and Indie is four. It is a Sunday, early afternoon, the rake too large for her, though she drags the wide mouth of its tines across an entire half of the yard, creating an impressive mound of brown, yellow, and orange from the tree, which, according to neighbors, is the largest one in the city, so our yard, by October, is weighed down with leaves. Stepping through them is like wading through knee-deep water. I am standing inside the living room, watching her, seeing the distance between us as far, though she is only a porch, a few steps, and half a yard away. The world outside seems separate, merely a projection I cannot connect with, like a painting in a museum that you know has nothing to do with what moves you. I put down what I'm sure is my second or third glass of Chardonnay, force myself to be present, go out and acknowledge her, and when I do, she asks me to jump in the pile. I tell her, "Not now," and I turn to resume my Chardonnay. "I'll be inside," I mumble to myself, "drinking."

When I'm done telling this story, Gary, my counselor, asks what I want to change when I go back home. I tell him, "I want to play in the leaves with Indie." He makes me write it down in the notebook I carry. "On the first page," he says, "so every time you open that notebook, you know why you are here." Gary, an alcoholic himself, had a degree in English, so he knew how important it was for me to write words down. Just now, I went to the hall closet to look at that page in the notebook, where I keep it in a box with all my other rehab writings, and I read the words, discovered the addition I had forgotten: "without hesitation."

Without hesitation. Elizabeth Bishop's command to herself in "One Art," "(*Write* it!)" comes to mind, so here goes: I am gripping the counter at the kitchen sink on the third floor of our family-housing apartment at the University of Colorado, staring out a window I have been looking through for months of nights when Kenny has not come home. I am holding on as hard as I can, because inside, everything is falling. It is as if I have stumbled on a precipice of a canyon on the moment of its collapse, my toes on the edge, my gut being pulled down by the gravity of a sudden, new reality. I turn and pace through the rooms of the apartment, stop briefly to throw myself across the new bed—the one we named the George W. because we bought it with our tax rebate money the year he thanked everyone with a $300 check—or I stumble against the walls into the bathroom, look at myself in the mirror to verify the fact that yes, this is me, and this is real—unable to stay still for fear that if I stop moving, then the reality of the moment will settle into the reality of my life. I go back to the sink, throw up, my feet even come up off of the floor, my weight thrust into my shoulders, hunched over the truth of this schism between the life I chose and the life I would now live. Wailing, I think, is the word for the sounds emanating from a place so deep I did not know it was a part of me, and now, as I write the moment, I realize since that morning, it has never gone away.

Kenny is behind me, in that brown thrift-store chair, where he has been sitting for two hours, he says, which means he came home at five thirty this morning. He keeps telling me to calm down, to stop screaming, that I am scaring the neighbors. Where was Indie that morning? I have blocked that out. Was she sleeping? No, she'd wake at six AM and never nap, never has, even now. She must have been somewhere else, because I would have never allowed myself such abandon with her in the apartment. He does not move from that chair, even as I rush through rooms, grip my stomach, white-knuckle the counter at the sink. Why did I keep going back to that sink? Sturdy, maybe. After all, the third-floor structure beneath me had encountered a ground swell, and I did not trust it. Kenny just sat there in that chair, the way the man in the Carver poem does, waiting for the woman to stop weeping. It is the chair where he cried after finishing Hemingway's *A Farewell to Arms*, and when I asked him that day why he was crying tears that seemed beyond the maudlin ending of a guy walking back to the hotel in the rain, he said he shouldn't have read it, that now he knew what it would be like if he ever lost me.

My tears that morning began at seven thirty and kept on, off and on, for years, but they had little to do with the failure of us, or what I assumed then was the failure of me. So I braced myself against the steepness pulling me down, knowing it was not mine, but Indie's. You see, I knew his leaving me meant that he was gone for good. He would not share custody, he would not call on Christmas or send cards on birthdays, he would vanish, poof, disappear, and I would stay behind and stand every day on the edge of that gaping hole beside her, hoping to make some sense of the landscape of absence she carries in the west of her heart. It was the moment I first realized I was Indie's mother, a single mother.

I am not a single mother who is divorced, because we never married. I am not a single mother who lives on welfare. I am not a single mother whose husband is in prison. I am not the single mother you pity. I am not a victim. I am not the single mother who has the kids all nights except Wednesdays and a week in the summer. I am not weak; in fact, no single parent has the cabinet space for weakness, or much cabinet space at all, for that matter. But I am not a cliché. I am a strong woman with four college degrees, including a doctorate, who loved a man with an intensity that distracted me from the truth, that he is the kind of man who leaves, and who, wherever he is now, will leave again. I am a woman who is raising our child by myself.

I am a single mother, one of many, many other mothers who hopes beyond hope that her child will never feel pain, but for Indie and me, as we have discussed during extended bouts of her questions, my answers, our shared tears, we live with an absence, or as she describes it, "a hole in her heart," one that is brought to attention every time a kid at school or a friend continues to ask, "You don't have a dad?" No. She has a father, a vanishing act, a magician who, with one tug of the gearshift on his truck in the parking lot, pulled an irreversible sleight of hearts.

Not long before Kenny drove away on that September Sunday, Indie was in the middle of the living room floor on her alphabet blanket playing with her toys, the monkey he named Spencer, the portable mobile she liked to play under, and she turned her head and looked at him. Holding her stare, Kenny said, "She's stronger than I am." I could feel it then, he was right. No matter how many times I write him, I find more words in the recesses of my memory, and those have just come back to me in the past few months. "She's stronger than I am." And now that she has grown into her own sense of self, I know he was right.

Indie's at the front door, beckoning me with her bright face to leave the words I am sifting through and come outside. She has been playing in the leaves every afternoon this week, raking them into a large pile until the sky darkens and threatens the end of her revelry, or I convince her to come inside with the words "hot chocolate on the table."

These are some things I would like to tell Kenny: Indie wears her yellow rain boots every day, even when the sun is out. She is now eight (Does he know that? Does he ever add it up in his head?), she has his build, his height, so that she and I are almost the same size now. She never wears an outfit without a peace sign on it. She designs her own haircuts. She can swim a mile without stopping, and she goes to a rock-climbing class every Saturday with her buddy, Jackson. She loves to read and draw and watch *Brothers & Sisters* with me on Sunday nights. That she and I live all of these moments together.

She is urging me to come out and see something before it disappears, blows away. I hurry out, see that she has created a circle of leaves, a circumference of brown and yellow and hints of deep red that almost covers our yard. She tells me it is a fort of leaves, and when I ask to come inside, she holds the rake like a guard, explaining that no one is allowed inside except for her and Blue, who, at that moment, runs out and intuitively leaps over the fort's imbricate walls.

Indie dances inside her fort, defies loss. She is dancing a ceremony of leaves, and I stand in the yard, clapping and singing a made-up song about the fort, without hesitation.

THE FICTION OF HISTORY

The front window of the duplex in Stillwater, Oklahoma, had
been smashed by a brick that was still in the garden. Inside,
the carpet had been stripped. I stepped around paint cans
and lazy drop cloths while the stout, curly-haired manager
assured me the owners would put in new carpet, paint the
walls, and install ceiling fans in both bedrooms. Then she
waved me out onto the porch. Maybe she worried that if I
stayed inside longer, I'd change my mind.

With Indie starting kindergarten in two weeks and the
classes I'd be teaching at the university less than a month
away, I signed the lease on the hood of the woman's small
navy truck. It was only then she seemed relieved enough to
explain that the previous tenants, a woman and her small
child, had left abruptly. "My god," she said, sliding the lease
into her binder, "there were toys everywhere. It was a mess."
I watched her look back toward the front door as if remem-
bering what she had seen there, and before I could ask, she
put her head down and shook it, her eyes closed in a gesture

that seemed to be part prayer. I asked when the window would be fixed.

––––––––––

Kenny and I used to play a game called People History. We'd take turns picking out strangers in public—like the stiff couple across the bar, the man talking to himself on Pearl Street, or the girl who lived in the apartment above us on Elder Avenue. Most of the time, he would be the one to pick someone and begin the story, and together we would weave an intricate, intriguing past. The story unfolded until it revealed how the stranger came to be at that place, that moment.

The years we lived in various cities and apartments to-gether, we had some neighbors with stories we knew, and others we didn't know at all, so we carved them from the fewest of details. The most mysterious was the girl who lived above us in Boulder. In the middle of almost every night, she vacuumed in a frenzy of geometric angles. I'm not sure we ever saw more than her brown curls poking out beneath the wool hat she pulled over her ears when she'd walk out to her car. This is what we knew: the wind chime, her white Honda, her phone ringing through rooms where she'd pace, and the way she dropped her hairdryer in the bathroom every morning. Once, we heard Sinatra from her open balcony door.

On the day she moved out, I watched from the kitchen window. I collected the details so that I could later tell Kenny: her corduroy jacket, the blue suitcase she lugged down the stairs, the thud at each step. The way she slipped in the snow and envelopes from the small bag she carried spilled onto our shared porch. She picked up each one with shaking fingers, and I leaned back from the windowsill, sure she didn't want a witness to her escape, which is what it looked like from where I stood. Our apartment felt emptier the day she drove away, and when Kenny came home hours later, his key in the lock was like a school bell ending recess.

———

In the duplex, Indie and I lived next door to an opera singer and a Marine. These were their stories: The opera singer wanted to graduate from OSU and stop working at Walmart. The Marine wanted to go back to Albuquerque to the wife who kicked him out, but mostly he wanted to get through one night of sleep without seeing the roads of Afghanistan.

———

One of the last afternoons I was in Boulder, I sat on a bench with my father in the hours following the final custody hearing, the one in which Kenny and I could not look at each other while we took turns on the stand. A friend of ours, the woman who introduced us years before, sat in the back row of the courtroom, and as we adjourned, she wiped tears from her cheek with a quick sweep of the back of her hand and said, "I keep thinking of how this story started, and I can't believe this is the way it ends." *It isn't ending*, I thought. *There will never be an end to this.*

My father and I sat together, looking down Pearl Street toward the mountains behind the Daily Camera building. It was his first time in Colorado, and after we sat for a time in silence, he said, "This is a beautiful place. You must really hate to leave." I sighed, kept looking in the distance toward the front window of my favorite bookstore.

———————

Indie chose the small bedroom in the duplex, but she never felt comfortable there. And after a few months, I stopped questioning her refusal to play or even sleep in it because I could feel it, too. It was as if some tragedy had taken place there, and no matter how many times we rearranged the furniture or added a tie-dye wall hanging, a new white nightstand, or a bright purple shag rug, the room trembled with an unknown story.

———————

The first place Kenny and I shared, the basement apartment in Fort Collins, was beneath a blue house, and the entrance was in the back. We had a large porch where we kept a *chimenea*, a camping chair, and a green recliner, my writing chair. It was where I came to know the sounds of our neighbors' afternoon sex.

We never saw them, those neighbors, only the sheer white curtains of their bedroom billowing from their open window. When Kenny came home from work, I'd point to the curtains, and we'd silently rush downstairs to our own bedroom and have sex as if we had to keep up.

In Stillwater, we all exchanged keys, knew each other's apartments. The Marine never locked his door, which was befitting, as he always had people coming and going because he needed the distraction. He repeatedly made remarks about his "self-medication" and moved through his rooms in a haze of imported beer and fine wine. Once, he told me it kept him far enough away from himself to get through the day.

When the harder stuff came out, his door would close. He'd emerge, later in the day or sometimes not until the next one, bleary eyed and squinting. As for the opera singer, she came outside to let her dog out or to bound down the front porch late for work. But I heard her all the time—singing, playing the piano, talking on the phone to friends—her voice, even when she wasn't singing, sang. Once I heard her through the wall of my bedroom wailing in her own. Even her crying was operatic, each gasp and release a clear, high note of pain that she held for as long as she could before the tone lowered into a crescendo of naked grief.

One night in Fort Collins while Kenny was out of town on a job, I slept through a fire that consumed the front porch of the blue house above us. The next morning, I found the two college boys who lived there standing in the front yard, dumbfounded and looking a bit guilty. I remembered seeing their makeshift ashtrays—stained coffee cups and pizza boxes—on a wobbly table out there a few days before. I wondered how I had slept through such emergency, why they hadn't thought to knock on our door and warn me to get out. But I also worried that the wine I had started drinking every night had dragged me into a sleep not even the sirens of a fire truck could shake. I shuddered at the many mornings I had gone into the living room to find the flames of candles I had forgotten to blow out before bed. I stood in the yard with the boys feeling like I had been called outside to see the damages I was hiding inside. The slats of the porch were charred, black, and its columns were bent like two arms struggling to hold something up.

A year or so after that fire, when Kenny and I moved to Boulder, something began to tear at the foundation of the life we shared, and I didn't sleep through it. In fact, I rarely slept at all—instead I waited all night at the window of our apartment—convinced that if I could stay awake until Kenny came home, I could save us from destruction.

———————

During the four years we lived in Stillwater, Indie and I planted periwinkles or begonias each spring in the garden. Indie liked to gather what we found buried in the garden, and I'd watch her carry piles of weeds and mysteries to the sidewalk. She always wore bright shirts with peace signs on them and mismatched socks—a turquoise sock with a yellow one, a green-striped sock with a white one with orange stars. When we'd stand together looking at our progress, she'd come a few inches below my shoulder. Kenny was over six feet to my five, and I had started to realize Indie would stand above me within a few years. She'd kneel down to spread more of the soil, and I'd watch her hands, the nails I had painted bright pink the night before already chipped and dirty, her bobbed blonde hair mussed in the back. Digging down, we'd uncover pull tabs, beer-bottle caps, slivers of glass.

The opera singer had a collage of pictures framed on a wall in her living room. All the pictures were from the 1970s: men with moustaches and sideburns, women with lingering beehives or long straight hair, kids in stiff collars and plaid jumpers. There was a couple, some grandparents, and one man in a turtleneck smiling off camera, the same man standing on a rock overlooking a canyon. The man was her father. He died when she was a few months old.

She told me the story on a night while we drank together on our shared front porch. I had become much more careful about my drinking, pouring myself a glass only if someone else was doing the same and always stopping long before everyone else did. It was important, I now understood, to manage my vulnerability, to be present for myself, for Indie, to no longer abandon both of us in the wine. The opera singer told me she felt as if she were half of who she was, and how she knew when a gesture or a facial expression, even a habit, was familiar when a certain look crossed her mother's face. A look of sudden recognition, remembrance. It happens to me when Indie moves her eyes a certain way, holds her mouth when she sleeps, moves through the rooms of the house with her shoulders held in a way I saw Kenny do countless times.

Kenny had been married before we met. His ex-wife called often, and her tones shifted with the seasons. I remember a message left on a New Year's Eve when we lived in Fort Collins, a wish for a good year in a sweet voice that made me feel something for her, and looking back now, I see it as foreshadowing, the warning that one day it would be my voice on the other end from miles away. By the time we moved to Boulder and I was pregnant, her tone altered with her lack of patience at his inability to keep up with alimony payments. According to the strictures of their divorce, he was responsible for half of the mortgage, the one for the house she now lived in alone in a state where he was wanted for failure to pay.

During our last winter together, the phone calls increased to an invasive level, some of them from her lawyers. Eventually, a warrant arrived in the mail. Every time the phone rang or someone knocked on our door, Kenny would panic, sure it was the police. One night, he went to the grocery store and took longer than expected. I worried he had been pulled over, picked up. I called, but his phone went to voice mail. And then, a knock on our door. I answered to find a man in a satin racing jacket and big black boots. Seven months pregnant, I pulled my robe around me as much as I could. The snow rushed down in diagonal lines, shining in the light from the parking lot. The man, an unkempt beard and a gold watch, stepped back a bit as if surprised. He asked if Kenny was there, and I said no. We both stood looking at each other for a moment as if trying to figure out the other's relationship to the man we both claimed to know. I shut the door and flipped the bolt.

Fiction and history are neighbors. The stories we tell about our own histories might as well be fiction—for what we tell, what we don't.

Not long after the Marine moved in, he invited me over for coffee. It was one of those conversations that includes the exchange of entire histories. He made the coffee in his French press, steamed the milk on a burner of his stove, sprinkled nutmeg. I took the oversized mug he offered and stretched out my legs on his couch. We both had the day off and could afford to sit in our pajamas on a Tuesday while he made two cups of coffee at a time.

He spoke of his ex-wife in Albuquerque, her nine-year-old daughter, the landscaping business that had exhausted him and their marriage. He complained about financial pressures and the struggle of being a stepfather. At one point, he got up and pointed out the photo booth strip on his refrigerator, the three of them huddled together, leaning close to the camera, laughing, wide-eyed. Was this all he had left? Photographs on a refrigerator? He missed them, wanted to go home, but he was here, working to get the college degree he had dismissed at nineteen and again at twenty-two when he enlisted. He was now thirty-one, divorced, a veteran of two tours in Afghanistan, and unable to sleep past five. As that morning slid into afternoon, we traded the coffee for Cabernet Sauvignon, but after one glass, I guarded myself against where I knew he was headed. I thanked him for the coffee and closed the door behind me.

————

Most of the time, the Marine talked about the classes he was taking, the latest college girl to fall into his bed, or the life he wanted to get back to in Albuquerque. But after hours or days of drinking, there always came a moment when he turned onto the road toward the hills of Afghanistan. It was either the bullet whizzing past his left ear during an ambush or the civilian family he and another Marine were ordered to execute. The darker the drinking hour, the more graphic the telling.

On that first morning in his apartment, I listened intently—the family in the car, the father who refused to stop at the post, his officer's command to "light them up"—and I heard the story as one of many in the makeup of his history, but as the months went on and he sat in his armchair or stood out on the sidewalk or slumped on the end of my couch and drank his Heinekens after I had put Indie to bed, I recognized that story as a shift, dark and dangerous.

His drinking pressed him down into the most jagged of edges, and his turns were always like a car approaching from around a corner. Even after he had turned to go back inside to his apartment or out the front door of mine, that darkness, it lingered, but I didn't mind it. I remembered my own dark nights from years ago, the jagged edges. I had no problem allowing him his.

And then there were those early mornings when I'd open the blinds of my front window to find him in the yard with his dog. The two of them jumping and dodging each other. His dog leaping and wagging, the Marine squatting down, grinning, freezing for a moment before pitching forward, hands raised, a game.

————

When Kenny left, he moved to a small mountain town outside of Boulder. We used to drive the thirty miles up the steep mountain road on Sundays to the same town for breakfast—orange juice and biscuits and gravy. After breakfast, we'd roam the aisles of the town's bookstore then stand out on its porch and imagine what it might be like to live such a simple life. Now he lives there with someone else.

————

The walls of the duplex were so thin that when the opera singer warmed up or practiced the aria she was to sing in her upcoming performance, we heard every note, every trill. When she played the piano, Indie and I would turn off the TV or put down our books and listen.

————

Kenny and I moved out of three apartments. The first was the basement in Fort Collins when I was five months pregnant. He was on the road working, so some friends helped me load a U-Haul to move to Boulder. There, Kenny built me a wall of bookshelves, painted Indie's room a pale yellow, and slept through the 9/11 attacks in our bed, even after I tried to wake him to tell him of the first plane and again, just after the second.

Those were the months I took a bus every morning to CU, the months he was out of work, the mornings I'd put on my maternity overalls while he slept in, the late afternoons I drove to the South Boulder Y to swim laps while he pored over want ads and the phone book. On February 1, twenty-two days before Indie was born, he came in one afternoon to tell me that the interview he had just had to be a maintenance man at a resort had gone really well. He also added that the receptionist noticed he wore no wedding ring and asked if he had a girlfriend. "I told her that you were pregnant," he said, "and she looked really disappointed." So did he.

By March, it was clear we couldn't afford the apartment we lived in, so we had to find another. During a snowstorm, we moved again, this time to the University's Family Housing, three flights up. That first night in our new apartment, after the last of the boxes and the lamps had been set down, we stood in the living room facing each other across from our mattress that leaned against the wall.

I moved out of that apartment alone after Kenny moved in with the receptionist. On the last day I lived there, I swept and scrubbed and mopped quickly, unwilling to linger in the rooms I knew I would always remember. I can still see the shine of the kitchen linoleum floor, the yellow paint in the second bedroom adorned by a border with elephants, giraffes, and hippos, and the gouged holes in the living room wall where my bookshelves had been. I can still see the telephone in the kitchen where I made too many calls begging him to come home. He did once, on an afternoon while Indie and I were out. I unlocked the door to find him on the futon. I carried Indie, in her car seat, just inside the door and set her down. I stood facing him, the door still open. He leaned forward.

"What are you doing?" I asked. I could tell he had just shaved. His goatee and hair were trimmed shorter than they had ever been, and he was wearing a T-shirt I had never seen. "Where have you been?" he looked worried. "I've been here for two hours."

I don't remember what I said.

"I missed you guys," he said, leaning back. I knew he meant it.

But he didn't miss us enough to come back for good. At some point, I got the nerve to ask for his key, a naive attempt to close the door between us.

———————

Eventually, the opera singer got a new job at Panera and worked the earliest shift, signaled by the *beep-beep-beep* of her Scion alarm that would rouse me from my sleep just before six in the morning, or the four o'clock afternoon shift, when she'd rush from her front door and off the porch a few minutes late in her khakis and polo shirt with her decorated name tag tucked into her purse. "Off to work," her singsong echoed, whether we were outside or not, and then, the three high beeps of her white Scion would sound again, the harmony to her departure.

When she was out of town, singing at a wedding or visiting her family, I'd go over to check on her dog or grab a roll of toilet paper, and I'd see the evidence of her struggle, blankets on a bedroom floor in front of a television, a mattress in the middle of the living room floor, a couch crowded with dirty clothes. But that was before I knew what might have thrown her into such fits of insomnia or days of shut doors and closed blinds, silence. I'd wander the rooms of her cramped apartment, slipping on the pages of an old syllabus, stepping over a single black Mary Jane and a jar of coins that had been spilled out onto the floor, apparently for quarters.

One afternoon, I opened the door to her refrigerator in search of a Diet Dr Pepper and found what I can only describe as a mega-minibar. Every shelf stocked: rum, vodka, an open bottle of White Zinfandel with the cork precariously lodged, banana liqueur, a box of Franzia, gin, and a syrupy grenadine barely capped. The bottles were layered four and five deep, and every bottle was the larger version, the magnums, the 1.5 liters, and not one of them full.

_____

One December in 2009, I came home from my last class of the semester to find an oversized envelope in my mailbox. I pulled it out to see a green Boulder County Court address in the top left-hand corner. I set my purse and book bag down on the porch and ran my finger beneath the sealed edge of the envelope. Indie would be stepping off the school bus at the corner within twenty minutes, and I had no idea what I might be told and no patience to wait for the first words in almost eight years.

I drew out a stack, pages. The first was a court order for a request to amend child support payments and in the five or six lines included for explanation, familiar printing: *See attached letter.* The large *S*, the singular line to cross both *t*'s, the period that seemed far away from its sentence. Kenny's handwriting. It was sunny that day, chilly.

The letter contained the history of the past few years of his life. His wife, his unemployment, their financial struggles.

Through the past eight years, I had imagined Kenny sitting near campfires in his Colorado mountain town drinking Bud Light and playing the guitar I had given him, laughing and being loud. Or he was driving to a concert in Aspen, moving along roads toward his next adventure, living a freedom he had chosen over fatherhood. But the letter told a different story, and when I told friends what the letter said, its details, they asked if it were true, suspected he had made it all up.

Standing on the porch, I read about a life I didn't know, and suddenly, the man I had been missing all those years fell away with every word and a new story began to take shape. His story.

In Kenny's version, I am Jill Talbot, a woman with whom he had a "short-term relationship" that resulted in an "unex-pected pregnancy." *My god,* I thought, *he makes it sound like I was a one- to three-night stand, not the woman he lived with for four years.* The story continues: I am the mother who took her infant to another state and asked not to be followed. No, I was the woman who fell apart in the living room and sobbed so loud the neighbors knocked on our door. I was the woman whose grief was so profound she could not stop calling him, could not stop smothering herself in Chardonnay. The story concludes: I am the woman he offered everything, the woman who wanted nothing.

We share a history, yes, but we tell competing versions of it: I wrote mine, again and again, the sad woman left behind with a little girl, trying to make sense of his sudden lack of feeling for fatherhood, for me, for the way we had been. Kenny told his story, shaping me into an uncaring woman who takes off and doesn't look back.

Dear Reader, I can't stop looking back.

For eight years, this is the story that had been told, and this was the first I had heard of it: an envelope in the mail, a two-page letter, and the truth: fiction gave him his freedom.

Change the story, and everything changes. In that moment, everything did. I no longer had to question why a woman would be with a man who had abandoned his family. She never knew. And I no longer wondered why Kenny's parents, who had driven nine hours from New Mexico to Colorado to the hospital when Indie was born, never stayed in touch.

My mind went back to scenes from the months surrounding his leaving that had confused me, and I could now read them through this new point of view. One I often come back to is the night Kenny borrowed a friend's truck and drove me to one of his friends' houses. He dropped me off without coming inside, which I thought was odd because it was his friend.

During the last months we were together, both of our cars had been repossessed, and I had been taking the bus to school.

He convinced this friend to sell me his car for only six hundred bucks, though it wasn't even worth that. And maybe it was Kenny's guilt that arranged for me to have a car after I had to move in with friends who lived an hour away from Boulder, where I had to be every day in order to finish school and teach my classes.

When I knocked on the door, a woman in a North Face pullover answered, and I told her who I was. She told me to come in then quickly turned away, leaving me standing in the open door. I stepped inside and carefully closed the door behind me. After standing awkwardly for a few moments, I sat down at a large dining room table. A clock ticked loudly from the wall in the kitchen. Then a bearded man came out with some paperwork and keys. The woman stayed behind him, standing as if they had somewhere else to be. I got up to shake his hand, but he ignored me and set the title transfer on the table. All I had to do was sign. Then he spun the paper around to his side of the table and signed it while I asked how long they had known Kenny and how much I appreciated them selling me their car. I remember my voice quivered from shame, from having to face what I thought were Kenny's new good-time buddies who got together and drank beer and played their guitars, while at home, I spooned sweet potatoes to Indie in her highchair.

"We've known Kenny long enough to think the world of him," the woman snapped at me. The man looked down at the table, shook his head, and made a sound like a grunt. Then the woman told me where the car was parked, and the man opened the door. I walked out into the dark.

When I got that letter, that night made so much more sense. To them, I wasn't a sad woman whose ex had been kind enough to leave her with a car. I was a heartless woman taking his child in it. No wonder Kenny didn't come inside—he couldn't risk the loss of his fiction.

Every Thursday morning, around seven, the trash truck stopped at our corner. Four forty-gallon blue plastic containers lifted, one at a time, by the mechanical arm of the truck and tilted, their contents spilling through the air. I watched this more than a few times, saw the past week of our lives falling away like water, as if such removal could cleanse us, allow us to start again, empty. Some mornings I'd still be in bed, hear the past week coming down, all the bottles—the Heinekens, the rum and the gin, a bottle or two of Chardonnay—colliding into a mass cacophony of clinking, breaking, shattering.

One night during the opera singer's rehearsals, Indie asked two questions: his name and if I had a picture. I was sitting in the chair. Indie on the couch. I stayed very still and told her his name. And while she readied herself for the picture of the man she only knew as Kenny, I went into my room and opened the closet that had a rumpled box labeled *Indie's Keepsakes*, where I kept my favorite outfits she wore as a baby, the baby book I had been given that was blank, and the dress she had worn the last time he saw her. I pulled the tape and dug through the soft yellow nightshirt, the tiny overalls, the checkered dress. I knew what I was looking for. The pewter frame.

I had kept it for her, the photograph of the two of us on the day we found out I was pregnant and we went camping in Poudre Canyon. We had placed it on a shelf in her nursery in Boulder. I got to the bottom of the box, and it wasn't there. I called out that I was still looking as I moved to the hall closet where I had a Priority Mail box labeled *Family Pictures*. It wasn't there. I rummaged through the drawers where I kept the custody documents, even went through the suitcase that held her sonograms. When I came back into the room to assure her I'd keep looking, I could tell we would not speak of it again for a long while. Next door, the opera singer held a note so long I almost lost my breath.

One night, years after we had been living in Stillwater, there was a forceful knock on our front door. Stillwater Police. I opened the door to a SWAT team and guns. I held up my hands, an instinct I didn't know I had.

"Marion Koby!" The one in front yelled while holding what appeared to be some kind of warrant. I recognized the last name from a peeling sticker next to the one that said "Talbot" on our mailbox.

"No. No." I yelled back as I moved in front of Indie.

"You're not Marion Koby?" The man, gun still drawn, held the piece of paper out and asked me to look at the name.

"No." Indie huddled behind me, more curious than afraid. Marion Koby had been gone from that address for over three years.

———

I gave the stout, curly-haired manager my sixty-day notice. During the last week of July, the U-Box I rented and packed had shipped, but I couldn't make myself pack up what would fit into the trunk of my car and drive away. As August neared, Indie and I slept on a comforter in the living room. All the walls were bare, the rooms empty save for the shower curtain and the rug on the bathroom floor. It wasn't that I considered staying; it was that I needed time to say good-bye to my story: the one that had me teaching four sections of first-year composition as a visiting professor and the one that had me still grieving over Kenny. Leaving was an attempt to leave both stories behind, and one was easy, already done. I was moving to a university where I would teach only creative writing. The other story, the one about Kenny, still lingered. The layout of this apartment I could leave, but the layout of my life, I feared, would follow me forever.

On the day I finally packed the car, I left cleaning supplies, a coffeemaker, a candleholder, and our plastic outdoor recliners, one blue, one green, the chairs Indie and I had carried out to the yard during so many late afternoons and early evenings. I left a note on the opera singer's door to go inside and take whatever she wanted. For the Marine, I left a six-pack of Heineken in the spot in our living room where he had sat so many nights.

I knew I would miss the leaves of the trees on our street, the way the night Oklahoma sky turns navy in August, the way Indie and I would lie in the plastic lawn chairs we bought and stare up at that sky, watching for nothing.

BOULDER COUNTY
CHILD SUPPORT ENFORCEMENT UNIT

Family Court in the State of Colorado
City of Boulder
Boulder County
Justice Center
1777 Sixth Street
Boulder, CO 80302

In the Matter Of:
███████████, Petitioner
against
Jill Talbot, Responder

CV-01-312
CN-0034-1204

Before: Elizabeth ███████, Judge

Modification Request Hearing Date: January 15, 2010

Judge: This is CV-01-312, and we're here today to discuss the
Modification Request submitted to the court on December 9,

2009, by Mr. ▇▇▇ in regards to the child support order that was established on June 23, 2003, in this court. Let the record show I did not preside over the original hearing, but I have read the permanent custody orders. Let me state for the record what those orders are. First, visitation, which includes alternating Christmas and Thanksgivings, along with five days visitation for the petitioner, Mr. ▇▇▇, each summer. As far as child support payments, a monthly payment is to be made by the non-custodial parent, Mr. ▇▇▇, in the amount of $634. Now, we have Mr. ▇▇▇ here in the court, and he has been sworn in, and he is without legal counsel. We have Ms. Talbot on the phone. Mr. ▇▇▇, you agreed to allow Ms. Talbot to appear in court via phone from Oklahoma, is that correct?

Mr. ▇▇▇: Yes. That's fine.

Judge: Okay, then, Ms. Talbot, do you have counsel?

Ms. Talbot: No.

Judge: Fine. Let's get you sworn in. Bailiff?

Bailiff: Please stand and raise your right hand.

She stands up behind her desk in her office on the fourth floor of the English building and raises her right hand.

Bailiff: Do you swear to tell the truth, the whole truth, and nothing but the truth, so help you?

Ms. Talbot: Yes, I do.

She sits down, imagines him sitting there at the table on the right side of the room, where he sat the last time they were in a room together. She holds the receiver of her office phone and holds on.

Judge: All right, is the visitation schedule still working out for both parents and Indie?

Ms. Talbot: There has been no visitation.

Judge: Hmmm, okay. Well, we're not here to discuss that today, so we'll move on. We're here to discuss the child support monthly payment as well as the back pay, so let's start with the monthly payment, which was set at $634. As I see in the records, these payments stopped being paid in December of 2003. Can you explain that, Mr. ███?

Mr. ███: When we went to court in 2003, I was making more money than I do now.

Judge: And according to the records, no payments were made after December of 2003?

Mr. ███: Right.

Judge: Why not?

Mr. ███: I couldn't make the payment, and I don't see Indie, so I don't think I should have to pay.

Judge: Mr. ███, I want you to understand something right now. As Indie's father, you have a responsibility, and, more so, according to this order, a legal obligation to support her financially until she reaches the age of nineteen. How old is Indie now, Mr. ███?

Mr. ███: Um, she's seven.

Ms. Talbot: She's eight.

Mr. ███: Oh . . . eight.

Judge: Let the record show that Indie is eight years old, not seven as Mr. ███ originally stated. Okay, according to your letter to the court and your financial statement, Mr. ███, you are currently unemployed. For how long?

Mr. ███: Off and on for two years.

Judge: But I'm looking at your most recent income tax return and see a payment of thirty-five thousand dollars, a new Ford truck, and a list of what appears to be construction equipment. This is income, Mr. ███.

Mr. ███: It's not . . . it's not income. That was a loan from my father-in-law to start my own construction company, and I'm currently paying him back.

Judge: You're paying him, what, monthly?

Mr. ███: Yes.

Judge: Well, Mr. ███, the court considers the amounts shown here, the value of the truck and all this equipment, as income. Ms. Talbot, have you received Mr. ███'s financial disclosure statement he was required to mail you before this hearing?

Ms. Talbot: No, I have not.

Thirty-five thousand is two thousand more than she makes in a year teaching four classes each semester.

Judge: I'll have a copy of these documents sent to you immediately. Now, Ms. Talbot, let's talk about your finances. Can we do that?

Ms. Talbot: Yes.

Judge: I have the documents you sent to the court with your current employment information, your last three pay stubs, and your most recent tax return. Mr. ██, do you have those documents before you today?

Mr. ██: Yes.

Judge: Good, let's proceed. I'm assuming Indie is in school. Private or public?

Ms. Talbot: Public.

Judge: Is she in child care before or after school?

Ms. Talbot: No, but sometimes if I have meetings or other university obligations, I take her to the Stillwater YMCA for child care.

Judge: And how often do you do that?

Ms. Talbot: Let me think. Probably five times a month.

Judge: And how much is that? Each time.

Ms. Talbot: Twenty-five dollars.

Judge: Okay, so let's round that up to $150 a month. You have health insurance for Indie, right?

Ms. Talbot: Yes, through the university.

Judge: Do you have any other source of income, Ms. Talbot?

Ms. Talbot: No.

Judge: Okay, I see here the deduction for family insurance on your pay stub. I also read in the original court order that you agreed to be solely responsible for Indie's health care. Would you like to change that? Do you want Mr. ▮▮▮▮ to begin sharing in those costs at this time?

Ms. Talbot: No, I can take care of that.

Judge: Fine. Let the record show I am looking at a copy of Ms. Talbot's pay stub from the fifteenth of December that she mailed to this court on December 17, 2009. Ms. Talbot, it shows your net salary of $1300. Is that monthly?

Ms. Talbot: Bimonthly, but I'm only paid for nine months.

Judge: Okay, let me see here, so that comes out to, hold on, divided by twelve. So you currently earn, on average, less than two thousand dollars a month?

Ms. Talbot: Yes.

Judge: And rent? How much is that?

Ms. Talbot: Four hundred and fifty.

Judge: Any other expenses beyond the usual bills?

Ms. Talbot: Student loans. I currently pay three hundred a month.

Judge: Mr. ███, Ms. Talbot, let me figure this for a moment.

She sits in the office, the door closed. He's a voice on the phone, *she thinks,* nothing more. *She's not sure why they're here, what difference any of this will make.*

Judge: Okay. Now, Ms. Talbot, I want to apologize to you for what I'm about to tell you, but right now, with Mr. ███'s employment status and the information he provided to the court about his current financial obligations, I am ordering him to pay the minimum amount required by the State of Colorado for child custody payments, and that's $400 a month. Now that's not much, but maybe it will make a difference for you and Indie.

Ms. Talbot: Yes, it will. Thank you.

Judge: Let's turn to the issue of back pay, which is, wait, let me look here, currently at forty-three, nearly forty-four thousand dollars. Ms. Talbot, this one is all up to you. Do you want to forgive this back pay?

She looks over at the red paper with the black scribbles in the frame on her desk. This is not her money; it's her daughter's. This is not her debt to forgive.

Ms. Talbot: No, I do not.

Judge: In that case, Mr. ███, I am adding twenty-five dollars to the four hundred. Now, Ms. Talbot, I know that twenty-five dollars isn't much against the amount owed, but I'm trying to get you some money and provide an amount that Mr. ███ will be able to pay. Okay?

Ms. Talbot: Yes, I understand.

Judge: Mr. ███, you are hereby ordered to pay $425 a month. You may make the payments direct to this court by the . . . what is today? The fifteenth of each month. Or you may send your payment to Ms. Talbot directly. Do you understand?

Mr. ███: Your honor, I can't make that payment.

Judge: Well you better figure out a way to make that payment, Mr. ███, because I'm being incredibly lenient with you today. In fact, before I let you leave this court today, I want you to make a payment of $425. Do you have a checkbook with you today, Mr. ███?

Mr. ███: Yes.

Judge: Good. Now, I'd like to revisit this case in six months because the minimum payment is unacceptable to me, as I'm sure it is to Ms. Talbot. I'll make a note to have the court send you both a letter with that information. Do either of you have any final statements you'd like to make before we adjourn?

Mr. ███: No.

Ms. Talbot: No, your honor.

Judge: Ms. Talbot, I assure you, we'll come back in six months and get this amount increased. In the meantime, I'm sending this modification order to the child support offices there in Payne County, Oklahoma. You can contact them if you have any questions.

Ms. Talbot: Thank you.

Judge: Court is adjourned.

Let the record show that the Payne County Office of Child Support in Stillwater, Oklahoma, has been the only state office to ever be successful in payment enforcement. After six months, a woman from that office called to tell her they received a letter from the Boulder County Court. According to the letter, the case was officially dropped by the State of Colorado because he no longer resides in that state. No payments have been received since, and his whereabouts remain unknown.

CANTON, NEW YORK

2011–2013

∎

THE PIECES

It's May, and she stands in a third-floor classroom in a building on a campus in northern New York. It took three flights to get here from Oklahoma. She reads from one of her essays, thinks of the way she bares herself for these strangers. She has lived in Stillwater for four years, longer than she has lived most places. But it's enough; it's time to go. She has become restless, wants not to start over, but to begin. She thinks of the way the word *may* means possibility, to be able.

The six-passenger plane bobs and dips over the green of northern New York, and she looks out over the trees, the farms, the winding rivers. She is on the way back to her daughter, to tell her that they will be moving to New York. Her daughter knows the pattern by now, how they live somewhere until they move to another. But this move feels different because it's not an escape. It's an opportunity. She'll be teaching at a prestigious private university for the first time, teaching the creative writing classes she's been working toward for years. She's not running away. She's running toward.

She rents a U-Box, eight feet by five feet by seven feet six, about the size of the bathroom in their small apartment. She will be able to fit everything they own into it after having a yard sale and selling the futon and some other pieces, and she will move her couch to one neighbor's, give her black writing desk to another. What she keeps is mostly her daughter's belongings: the wood bed frame, the mattress, the white nightstand, her polka-dotted bedding. She wants her to have these things, a consistency. She also keeps the vintage kitchen table and blue chairs she bought a year ago at an antique mall. She looks forward to the way it will now sit in a kitchen instead of being squeezed against a wall in the living room. Her vintage trunk is the first thing she carries into the pod. She uses it to store extra blankets and games—Connect Four, Scrabble, Uno—ones she and her daughter play together in restaurants. They have done this for years, the two of them sitting across from each other, setting up their game, the servers stopping by to ask who is winning. She heaves the mattress, slides in the bed frame, stacks boxes of pots and pans, dishes, and her books into the pod during one of Oklahoma's longest hundred-plus-degrees streaks.

The last two pieces are the bikes, the ones they ride every afternoon to the university swimming pool. When the pod is filled, she pulls the door shut. She lets her daughter hook the lock through the loop and secure it. The box will be shipped to New York the next morning, and she and her daughter will begin the fifteen-hundred-mile drive, passing through seven states over a period of five days.

They will stay in a Motel 6 in Indiana, a Super 8 in Ohio, a Holiday Inn Express in Buffalo. On the last night, they will be the only occupants at a Travelodge in Polaski, New York, only ninety-two miles from their new home in Canton, New York. She will decide they need to stay one more night, swim in the hotel pool, read in the sun, pretend they are vagabonds wandering the country. She wants to linger between here and there.

The next afternoon, they pull into the long gravel drive and get the keys out of the mailbox. She lets her daughter unlock the front door, and they step up into house, rush from room to room, wonder what they will do with all of this space. They bring their suitcases inside, put them in the back bedroom, roll out their sleeping bags on the living room floor, and plug in the small television. She thinks of the way she wrote a similar scene, one of the house in Utah, years before: "The first time I walked through the spacious house, I didn't see possibility or a new start. I saw a big, empty space. Those rooms looked like all I did not have, every room a challenge." She does not feel that way here. She embraces the sparseness. The emptiness a clearing.

That first night, she steps outside onto the back deck, her phone in her hand. She has not heard from him since the hearing a year and a half ago, but she still knows his number, dials into the dark. She wants to call from out here, not bring him into this house. According to the court, she must inform him of every move, every address change, and, even though he follows no orders, she complies. Such futility, she thinks. Adhering to her side of the order, the one she always keeps tucked away in a box, feels like calling the number of a house where she once lived and hearing that it's been disconnected. The ringing cuts to voice mail. She speaks out toward the trees behind the house, wonders if he'll write down what she tells him, knows it makes no difference where the two of them live. Or how. When she says the words *New York*, she feels the distance, the faintness of her feelings for him like the smoke from a firework that quickly fades, the blank sky where there had once been a bright explosion.

She hangs up, turns to go inside, finds her ten-year-old daughter in the back room leaning over her suitcase, searching for her toothbrush. She looks at their bags on the floor, the disarray that will eventually settle. In two weeks, their suitcases will be on shelves in the garage along with a few boxes, ones she never opens but carries from house to house. In one of those boxes, there is the photograph she'll find while unpacking.

EMERGENT

When I was eight, my mother and I were in our driveway in Lubbock, Texas, just back from some errand when she suddenly yelled, "GO!" and shoved me toward the garage and through the back door into the house. When I think back on it, I see myself flying in that moment from the edge of the garage's opening to the house. Once inside, I ran to my parents' bedroom. Soon my mother was there, shaking, muttering, "No. Oh, no." She called someone, asked for an ambulance, said there had been an accident. She told me to stay inside, to not look out the windows. Not long after, I heard sirens. And the sirens, it seemed, kept coming. It's been more than thirty years since that moment, and I can still feel her strong push. I can even hear the crash and the shattering of glass I never heard.

I usually wake by ten o'clock on Sunday mornings, but this Sunday was different. From my bed, I could see through the hallway to the bathroom, where Indie was leaning over the black rug toward the toilet. She was sitting on her feet, her hands on her knees, as if she'd been running all night in her sleep and had woken in recovery mode. It was the end of October, and this was not the first time I had found her here, vomiting into the toilet. Her bobbed hair sticking up in the back, tousled, blonde. I asked if she needed me, hoped that she didn't, because I was exhausted, my head tight, pounding. I wondered how the one glass of Chardonnay I had the night before had settled in so heavily.

We had only lived in the house since August, so Indie didn't yet have a pediatrician. The week before, the pharmacist at the Price Chopper suggested Pedialyte, maybe Ensure if she didn't start eating more. Fiber, he suggested. She'd be fine.

For weeks, I had packed a plastic grocery bag and an extra set of panties in Indie's backpack for school, fourth grade that year, and each time, she brought home the soiled pair in the bag. She'd set it on the top step in the basement, and I'd take them down to the washing machine, toss them in, and rush back up the stairs.

Our house faced Main Street, also Route 11, a large parenthesis that curved through mid–New York state. The traffic was steady. When I stood in our yard against the rush of speeding trucks, I could see the flags at the campus entrance, stretching or bowing in the wind. I had never lived in a house with a basement, and the orange glow of the furnace unsettled me.

When Indie gets home from school, we have reading time. Indie on the garnet loveseat, me on the matching couch. That fall, whenever I looked up from my book, her head would be on the pillow, her eyes closed, a blanket pulled up around her, even when it was September. She'd sleep as long as I let her. She was tired, weak, not hungry, this girl of mine who never took a nap, even when she was a baby. I couldn't concentrate, felt the pull of sleep. Within a page or two, even I gave in. An hour, sometimes two. Waking up at five o'clock in the dark of a North Country fall hurt, but Indie's homework had to get done, and I had to make dinner.

At the Price Chopper, I'd buy three Gatorade quarts at a time, sometimes not leaving the parking lot before opening one and gulping in relief. We were thirsty, exhausted.

If she wasn't better tomorrow, I told Indie, I'd take her to a doctor.

———————

The night after my mother pushed me into the house, I remember pulling back the heavy curtains in my bedroom, seeing in the glow of the streetlight the glitter of broken glass in the front yard. Waiting for the sirens, my mother had talked nonstop: the black car, the green car slamming into its side, the car hurtling above our yard. She could not stop herself from telling it, as if it were a secret she'd just learned. She wasn't talking to me. Sitting on the navy comforter of my parents' bed, I watched her lithe frame in the mirror above the dresser. I can still see the thick brown carpet with gold flecks, the nightstand behind her. The secret kept.

———————

My mother's childhood home in Mt. Pleasant, Texas, had been a cacophony of chimes from the dozens of grandfather clocks lining the hallway and the clinks of glass behind a closed door during her own mother's all-night benders. She spoke about her childhood only in flashes, hints my father and I would try to catch like fireflies. She had been a sleepwalker as a child. Once, her father found her on Highway 67, which ran in front of their house. She was in her nightgown, standing in the middle of the road as if waiting to be hit.

That morning, Indie stood in the hallway between the bathroom and her bedroom as if testing her bearings, and I told her to climb into my bed where I could keep watch without having to move myself. She told me her head hurt, and I asked if it was knocking like mine, then rubbed her back until she fell asleep. We'd sleep till we felt better, or at least rested. It was already past one o'clock in the afternoon. After five mornings of getting up at 6:45 so that she could be ready for the bus, we'd sleep in on Saturdays, Sundays, but never that late, never past ten.

It was the move itself, I thought. The drive from Oklahoma to New York, the new place, the new house. Seven states in five days. For weeks, we slept side by side in the living room in sleeping bags on the hardwood floor, the rooms of our new house spacious, hollow. When our moving van arrived, ten days later, we carried every piece of furniture, every box of books, every lamp and rocking chair through the front door.

Mrs. Carter told us that Stacy Green had broken her arm in a car accident and that her father had died. We would be making cards for her that afternoon during Reading. I stared at Stacy's empty seat, thought about raising my hand to say that she and her father had crashed into my front yard, but I didn't. The house pictured on the cover of the *Avalanche-Journal* was mine. It would make me responsible somehow for what had happened, for the shattered windshield, for Stacy's arm snapped between the door and the window crank, for the bloody figure I imagined crumpled in the grass.

Indie bolted out of bed and rushed toward the bathroom but didn't make it. This was not the first time, so I knew the routine—first the paper towels, then the wet towels, then the cleanser, the washing machine, the rush up from the basement. I helped her clean up, got her a new pair of panties—her favorites, the ones with the monkeys on them—then guided her back to bed. My head a weight not centered with the rest of my body, so much that I kept both hands on the bed as I moved around to my side, crawled back on top of the covers.

By the end of September, Indie was going through four pairs of panties a day, the diarrhea explosive, sudden. When she began to look ashen, I asked a colleague to recommend a pediatrician. Indie sat on a chair in the waiting room, huddled in her heaviest coat. The doctor was not accepting new patients, the receptionist said, and gave me the name and number of a pediatrician in Potsdam, ten miles east. I tried to argue. "Please, she's so pale," I said.

"You could take her to the clinic downstairs, but it won't open until four." She looked at Indie. "She might need help before four, so you could take her to the emergency room," she said. Then she closed the window.

The house we rented from the university had two stories, a basement, and a two-tiered back deck. The front door was red, the house cream. A large tree hovered out front, a stone walkway leading from the driveway to the front porch. Indie once said it was the kind of house you want to draw. The kitchen was spacious with a yellow countertop, an electric stove, a window over the sink that looked out to the backyard. There was no air-conditioning in the North Country, so through August and early September, we opened every window, let the eighty-degree wind through the screens.

Indie was up again, this time in the hallway, and when I asked what she was doing, she said she was going to get some Cheerios. I closed my eyes, relieved that she was up, moving about. Maybe I'd sleep for just a bit more and join her, watch the political talk shows I'd taped. I fell asleep again, then heard her, sniffling. She was back, standing in the doorway, sobbing. "I can't do it," she gasped. "I can't get to the kitchen. I'm too dizzy."

"Lie down," I told her. "I'll rub your head so you can sleep." My hands fumbled in her hair. Food poisoning. Surely.

It was hot in my room, and Indie and I tossed off the covers. The vent near my bed blew warm air, as if it never

shut off during the night. I got up, checked the thermostat, sixty-eight. I lowered it to sixty, stumbled back to
bed, wondered what was wrong, why the furnace blew all
night against the thermostat that told it to shut down at
sixty-five.

When August slipped into September, the leaves covered
our yard, and we'd wade through them as if dragging our feet
through a stubborn river. We settled in, learned the rhythms
of the sun that set before we were ready. The dark was quick
here. Moving from room to room, we lowered the blinds.
September was in its final weeks, and the thermometer on
the living room wall read fifty-five. I pressed a button, felt
the rumble of the furnace in the basement.

At the clinic, the physician's assistant, a stout woman in
jeans and a blue North Face jacket, diagnosed Indie with a
stomach virus. One had been going around. For a moment,
she leaned against the sink looking at both of us, first one and
then the other, as if second-guessing her easy diagnosis. If
she stops drinking or if her tongue looks like that again, she
finally told me, take her to the emergency room.

By one thirty, I made myself get up, felt my way along the
wall in the hallway to the kitchen. We needed to eat something. Protein would help. I got out the turkey bacon, set a
paper towel on a plate, picked four eggs from the carton. It
was heavy in the house, a weight bearing down. I turned from
the yellow countertop to the stove and fell, a puppet suddenly
released from its strings. I tried to stop what was happening,

put one elbow on the counter and one on the stove, but the tile pulled me toward it, and I went down.

I woke up on the kitchen floor, the stove moved from its place against the wall. I must have held on to it like an anchor, dragged it across the tile as I fell. I had to get up, get back to Indie. The eggs barely whisked in the black bowl, the turkey bacon in the microwave. I left it all, but not before turning off the coffeepot. Before I could get back to bed, a sudden sweat shifted to a chill, and I crawled beneath the covers and pulled them up over my shoulders, sure that sleep would stave off this sickness.

Within minutes, the room swelled in heat, and I broke out into a sweat. Indie's hair was wet, sticking to her neck. We needed rest, to sleep as long as we could, but Indie slept too soundly. She'd fallen down into a depth, and I had to stay awake, on watch, in case she slipped further away.

I turned over, put my hand on Indie's back to feel her ribs rise and fall. The sun through the slats in the window blinds seemed separate—as if we were hidden there, invisible, under a heaviness I could not attribute to wine, to a long week, to a late night. Indie seemed elsewhere, and I watched her in that moment against all the other moments of her sleeping: Her arms raised above her head in her crib—how I came to understand this meant complete surrender, exhaustion. Her head lolled over to her right shoulder in her car seat, her steady breaths above the hum of the highway. Her mouth agape in the morning's moments before I woke her, her eyelids that never closed completely so that I could read the rhythms of her dreams. This sleep was a closing down, a curling in, and I willed myself to break through the brace that held me to that bed, that room. Something was wrong, and I knew we had to leave. Get help. But first, the house.

What happened next was methodical, trancelike. First, I went back to the kitchen. Poured the eggs into the sink and rinsed the bowl, wrapped up the turkey bacon, rinsed the coffeepot. Next, I went to Indie's room and made her bed. In the bathroom, I washed my face, brushed my teeth, refolded the towel and draped it on the rod next to the sink. In the living room, I folded the beaded throw over the back of the loveseat. I stepped from room to room, stood at each door for a final inspection, remembered what my mother taught me: *Leave the house neat. If something happens to you and you never come back, you want people to find the house nice.*

My mother picked up every glass, every bowl, every pair of shoes as soon as they were set down. Growing up, I had to make my bed before leaving my room. Every time we'd leave the house, all the lights were turned off, the throw on the couch folded just right, my shoes placed on the floor of my closet. My mother's insistence on control, I think, was a way to reverse her own mother's chaos, a worry that anyone might come into their house and find (as she once did when she came home from school) empty bottles around the living room, vomit draped over the sink and the back of the couch, her mother sprawled naked and passed out in the back bedroom after a day of drinking. She kept things put away because so much had been left out, undone, by her own mother. That afternoon, before we left the house, going around to each room was a ritual that would not bear interruption. It was also the only time I looked at our house the way a stranger might, saw how they would see us through the rooms of our house, our home. I understood what my mother had meant: the house was us. But I was about to learn something she had known all too young, that no matter how nice you might keep your house, something beyond your control can destroy the depiction, seep like poison.

———————

The hospital was right across the street from our house. I took Indie's hand, and we worked to steady each other, ourselves. I told her we could make it. Indie collapsed before we made the sidewalk, heaved into the grass of our neighbor's yard. Neither one of us could stand, our legs a betrayal. I sobbed and stumbled toward the street, waved my arms and called out for help, the cars on Route 11 speeding by.

A blue car slowed to a stop. Inside, a woman smoking a cigarette and a teenage boy listening to music through the wires coming from his ears. She looked back to their backseat layered in shopping bags, empty soda bottles, and clothes. I let Indie in first, then crawled in, carefully, after her. The air in the car was as heavy and suffocating as our house. I guided the woman to the back entrance of the hospital while Indie sat so close our shoulders touched. I patted her leg, my hand trembling.

———————

Later, as we were being wheeled out of the clinic, Indie on a stretcher and me in a wheelchair behind her with an oxygen tank in my lap, I thought of the furnace, blowing and churning through the days, the nights, the months. Carbon monoxide poisoning. It seemed simple enough. How had I missed it?

The hospital turned out to be an after-hours clinic, so we were driven to Potsdam. "I'm right here," I told Indie as they wheeled her from the clinic and into the ambulance. The EMT led me to a seat and buckled me in next to Indie. I patted her on the arm, told her we were fine. From the window of the ambulance, I could see our house. It was strange, seeing it from the outside. The tree out front sheltering the porch, the accent of the red door belying the danger within. I thought about all the signs I had missed, Indie's diarrhea, our exhaustion, my inability to concentrate. My assumptions that it had been the cross-country move or adjusting to a region so different from the ones we had known allowed me to dismiss our struggles, or at least wait for them to dissipate, the way sand does when you step into a river. It rises up, expands, but then it falls back into itself, stills. I kept thinking that we were like that sand, and that within a few months, we too would come back to our selves. Our house, I assumed, was our haven, a sanctuary that kept us as we settled in to an unknown place.

My mother never considered her childhood home a haven or a sanctuary. After all, she spent most nights trying to escape it. But when she had a home of her own, she created one. I felt secure there. Even when cars crashed together just outside of it, I ran as far into the recesses of the house that I could, knowing I would be safe. The back room not a closed-off, clinking dungeon, but a place of protection, where I never had to worry. As it turns out, the house Indie and I escaped had a dungeon of its own—a furnace with a split chimney that unknowingly spread its poison through the rooms, through us.

I thought of how I had done everything I could to make a safe and stable home for Indie and myself, but there was a gaping hole in the chimney no one knew about, and it is there where the danger seeped out, crawled through every room, held us hostage.

I've never asked my mother if she remembers that car crash, and through the years, I've gone back in my memory, tried to separate what I know from what I imagined. If we are told stories about the past enough times, we begin to believe we were there, and my mother has put enough pieces of her childhood together for me that I can see the glow of the porch light from the front steps of that white house in East Texas. Looking back to that afternoon in Lubbock, I see my mother's frame in the mirror, the blur of the kitchen as I ran by, the black skid marks I found in the street the next morning on my way to school. What I don't see is what I wrote on my card to Stacy or the day she returned to school, if she did.

Memory forms, piece by piece. Some pieces go missing; others interlock, firm. We fill in the missing pieces with what we imagine or just leave the gap, admit the blank. And sometimes, we imagine what might have been, would have been. I do this. I still wake in the middle of the night, imagine the outcome if we had stayed sleeping. It's a jolt, like that moment when my mother pushed me into the house. Such near escape.

———

Hours later, Indie and I would sit in the lobby of the ER waiting for a taxi to take us home. While she watched *SpongeBob* on the small television in the corner, I stared at the brown and white tiles of the floor. If it's true we see our lives more clearly after we almost lose them, I saw that night for the first time that if Indie and I had died, Kenny wouldn't know it. I thought about all the times when Indie was in pain, in danger, in the hospital, and he had no idea. I understood, finally, how truly removed he was from our lives. We were on our own.

DREAM HOUSES

There's a man who walks up and down my street in a red T-shirt, jeans, and flat sneakers. Every few steps, he stops and looks back for a moment, then turns around, keeps walking. Slowly. The first time I saw this, Indie came into the kitchen to tell me there was a man outside, standing at the sidewalk, staring at our house. I went to the window, thinking of Kenny, always worried that one of these days, one of these years, he's just going to be there. It's absurd, really, that I think this way. It's been ten years.

———

When Indie and I lived in Utah, I'd dream of Kenny outside our house, his figure standing out on the sidewalk, a threat wanting inside. But during those years, I also dreamed of a large building, a warehouse it seemed to be, and the two of us were always in the back of it. We were behind a vast space, high walls, and he'd ask, again and again, if he could come back. Or he would be about to ask. In the dream, I wanted him to, and I didn't. I was dreaming an indecision. I never answered him. Sometimes I'd dream it for nights in a row, see us in the same position, crouched down and close, as if we were hiding. And the space we were in was different every time, but the dimensions remained. A large building, emptied, though it had once, I knew, been full of inventory. I'd wake up from it, frustrated at dreaming him again, say, "Go away," to the dark.

This morning, Blue began to bark wildly at the window. I got up from my writing desk and went to look, and there was the man again, this time on the other side of the street, walking and pausing, looking back. I watched him do this until I couldn't see him anymore. His movements are a combination of expectation and escape, and it's difficult to tell what it's more like, because when he turns, it's quick, a pivot, as if someone has called his name. But his stance is impatient, as if someone, or something, follows. I've been moving this way, too, living in seven states in the past ten years. Escaping. Expecting. A few steps forward and something calls me back and I turn for a moment, and in a few more steps, I do it again. It's like a recurring dream.

My parents have lived in the same house since I was nine. I remember when it was just a concrete slab and a brick fireplace. During the past few years, my mother has replaced the beige carpet with hardwood floors, which makes the living room feel like a large cave. Our footsteps and words echo. It's like walking through the house of a neighbor who shares a floor plan: the layout is familiar, but the details are all wrong. I would prefer to have the house remain as it was in 1979, but the gold carpet in the dining room is now buff, the dark shutters on the front windows are gone, and the tiny roses of my bedroom wallpaper have been replaced by paint the color of buttermilk. The entire house is held together by reds: the chair and ottoman in the living room, the towels in the back bathroom, the pillows on my parents' bed.

Since my mother made the changes, I have dreams that I'm behind the house, either in the garage or at the back gate of the wooden fence, and I have no way of getting inside. The door has no knob, or the gate's latch is firm. It's as if I want to be let in, be allowed to come back to myself.

My father likes to drive by the other houses where we have lived in that town. The first one is a small house on Caladium Street, where I lived as an infant. Of course, I have no memory of living there; it's like a novel I never read. The other house, the one on Eastbrook Drive where I lived until I was five, I remember, but my father drives by to show me as if I don't. Every time, I sit in the backseat and look out the window, see this as the house I ran away from when I was four, when I grabbed my little red wagon and rolled it down the sidewalk. By the time my father caught up to me, I was on the median of a high-traffic street. He scolded me for leaving.

I have a pattern of returning, of going back. I left and returned to Lubbock four times, spending a total of nine years there. I left Colorado and went back, and I left Stillwater, Oklahoma, after a year and a half of graduate school in 1997 and returned ten years later.

The first time in Stillwater, I lived on the right side of a duplex on Washington Avenue. It had large windows that opened by cranking a lever, scratchy brown carpet, and a wraparound kitchen.

Twelve years later, Indie started first grade three blocks from that duplex.

Coming back to Stillwater was like a remembered dream, and I had to set the scenes—the steps of Morrill Hall, the booth of a favorite restaurant, a second-story apartment on Walnut Street—against what I remembered. It was like living a palimpsest.

But during the years of my absence, not all had remained. The university had purchased the land south of campus and razed all the duplexes and houses, including the ones on Washington. Yet nothing had been done to the area. It was all gravel and dust. For years, I had kept a picture of the tree in that yard on my refrigerator. Now there wasn't even a stump, and when I'd drive by where it had once been, I'd slow down, search for any trace of the tree, the sidewalk. I was driving by an absence, so I filled in the gaps and imagined the front windows, the blue bookshelf in the corner, the candle on the counter's edge, the heavy couch I left on the day I moved out.

At my going-away party held in that duplex, a friend brought a bottle of L'Ecole No. 41. It was a white wine; I knew nothing more. That night, I traded in my Bud Light bottles for a glass. In the nights after, I'd pack boxes on the

JILL TALBOT

living room floor listening to Counting Crows, sipping wine. Chardonnay, then, was an unwinding, an easy glass or two while listening to "A Long December."

For years, I searched the racks of every liquor store I entered, looking for the label: a white background with a crayon drawing of a school, a hot air balloon, and the sun. I remembered nothing more. A decade later, that label no longer exists; the winery traded the crayon drawing of a school for a sepia photograph of one. How symbolic, this transition from innocence to experience and the truth: things like wine labels and duplexes no longer remain except in the cellar of memory.

During the final semester of my PhD program, one of the professors in the English department, Dr. Morgan, made a phone call from Santa Fe to the chair to say she had decided to pursue her art and would not be coming back. When I had left town that May after graduation, I had a similar assumption, that the years in and out of Lubbock had finally come to a close, and all the men I had complicated there were best left alone.

It was sudden, unheard of, really, the way Dr. Morgan abandoned her job and phoned in a resignation. Some felt that my sojourn to wait tables in Colorado for a summer after completing a PhD was equally careless, so it was suggested I apply to replace her.

I did apply, but by the time I drove to Colorado and started working at the Dancing Bear, a Grateful Dead–themed restaurant specializing in Jewish fare, after I met Kenny and stayed up nights talking and drinking Shiner Bocks on the back porch that looked out over the Eagle River, I was as far from professorland as I could be, and the closest I came to using my education was when a busboy at the Bear who called me Dr. Jill had me write down book recommendations on napkins. It was a simple summer. The phone call I received from the department chair ended it, and I packed up my Jeep and drove back to Texas. My leaving Lubbock, as it turned out, had once again been temporary, and when I returned, I unlocked Dr. Morgan's office door.

All of her things remained inside. Standing in the midst of it, I understood what real leaving looked like. When she called to say she was not returning, she meant it. She had not packed up, had not sent for her things, had not turned in her keys. The first-floor office looked like it did the last day she had walked out of the door and locked it behind her. It took me several afternoons to remove her boxes of files, empty her drawers, take down the framed poster (from a Santa Fe Art Festival) and photographs from her wall, remove the cartoons and postcards from her door, replace her name with mine.

I had no inclination that this would be something I would do in my own life six years later, when I would write a last-minute resignation letter during the final week of a semester in May and leave Utah.

Back then, when I thought of Dr. Morgan, her going was a forward act, a pursuit—of her art, of the man she had reportedly mentioned in her phone call. I never considered, until that May in Utah when I did my best impression of her, that she might have been leaving rather than going. I'm thinking of how the word *forgo* means to omit or decline to take, and how in her going, for the sake of going, she had forgone. But what if hers, like mine, had been a declining so severe that she, that we, left everything behind?

I dream of this office, this hallway, this building often. It was torn down the year after I left Lubbock for the last time, but in my dream, I still roam from one room to the other—a classroom on the second floor, the main office (I go there often), my office, up and down the stairs. It always seems I'm looking for someone who has just left the building, just stepped out of the office. What if I'm dreaming the me that keeps leaving, keeps forgoing the rooms out of restlessness, or fear?

In almost every dream of the building, I go into the main office to check my mail, and my mailbox is full. I have to bundle it all in my arms and balance out of the office, worried I'll drop it all, that a close-passing colleague (there is always at least one) will see what I am holding, read the words I'm hiding. I've also had dreams of carrying large stacks of books from that office. Maybe I'm roaming the rooms because in that building, I traded one man for another like library books, and when I went back after that summer I spent with Kenny, I continued to check one out, return another. Perhaps the mail is all of my secrets that were torn down the day they razed that building, and the books the weight of my guilt, the apologies I think every day but never write.

Recently, I looked up Dr. Morgan, found a website that features her mosaic art. I wonder if she ever takes a piece of tile in her hand and places it in the variegated pattern, considers it the piece of her life she left behind in Lubbock.

I have a friend who has a recurring dream of her first apartment in New York City. In those dreams, every time she comes back to the apartment, there are additional rooms. In the first of those dreams she found her dog, who had died ten years earlier, old and bloated, but alive. He was lying on a narrow bed in a small, book-lined room that was closed off by a curtain she'd never noticed before. In some of those dreams, the apartment goes on and on, from room to room, sparsely filled with old furniture, carpets on the wooden floors, light streaming in from windows. Each time she finds that dream again, the rooms expand, go further and further back, and once came around in a circle. She's also dreamed of trying to get back to that apartment and not being able to find it, or when she does, it's not the place she'd left behind only a little while before.

What we leave won't leave us, it seems, the same way that Kenny won't seem to leave me, even though he did long ago. I can run from room to room for the rest of my life. It won't stop him from coming back.

For years after I moved out of the house in Utah, I dreamed it. In one, there is no furniture in the living room, and I can see through the sheer curtains of the two windows, and the front door is open. In another, I am in the kitchen, surrounded by chairs, boxes, lamps, appliances. All the cabinets are open.

I'm at the end of packing for a move, trapped by what I must leave behind. There are more dreams of this house: The one in which I open the front door and the porch has been removed, a gaping hole in the ground, and I stand on the edge of it, sure I'll fall. The hole is jagged and dark. It looks as if an excavator clawed into the ground. Even in the dream, I understand that this really is how that porch was for me on the mornings after those Chardonnay nights: the emptied bottles, the left-behind glass, an ashtray, the phone. No matter how much I tried to piece together the puzzle, I could not excavate the evening. All of those nights blacked out.

I haven't dreamed about the house for a couple of years. Perhaps I have gone back enough to the emptiness I felt in the living room, the opening of a refrigerator door each evening, the black hole of memory.

―――――――――

Disarrangement seems to be common in our dream houses. A friend e-mails that the most memorable location in his house dreams is the apartment he lived in until he was eleven. In the dream he usually finds it updated or more or less the way it looked in 1988. He also remembers dreams about being at a friend's house in Chicago's Hyde Park. It was a very big house with "all these staircases" and smaller rooms that connected larger ones. It had multiple floors, and only three people lived there (along with some Rottweilers that stayed primarily in the kitchen), so there were many unused areas. There was "lots of dust and ancient memorabilia" everywhere, and in parts of those dreams, he's going through passageways, finding old newspapers. That last sentence he ends with a question mark. He's also dreamed about the apartment where he lives now. Usually it's changed in some way, expanded. Something strange has happened to the design.

My grandmother died one week before her ninety-fifth birthday in October of 2009. During the last few years of her life, she'd ask what I wanted in the house. She'd suggest I make a list, tell me what my cousins had already claimed, say she didn't like to think of all of her things sitting in the house after she was gone. Perhaps she feared an estate sale, her things auctioned off to strangers, the way my other grandmother's belongings had gone, leaving me to wonder who now sits in her faded yellow chair with the cigarette burns, who rolls over at night into the depths of the feather bed I slept in as a child.

The large rooms of my grandmother's house were unused in those final years except for her bedroom, the TV room, and the kitchen, and I'd walk through the house looking at the photographs of our family, reading titles of the books in my grandfather's study. I'd pull one or two down, each time, find his underlines, the notes in the margins, the subjects of his sermons. My grandmother told me how my grandfather spent hours in his study preparing for Sundays, the light she'd see along the bottom of the closed door, the sounds of his typewriter.

During the final months of her life, she was too weak, too dizzy to do much but rest on the couch, so I'd sit down on the floor beside her, hold her hand. She'd tell me how my grandfather and his sisters had stood, just that morning, in the corner of the living room, or how the night before, two of her brothers (she had three, only one still living) came to the foot of her bed, asked "Sis" to come home. Doctors and other family members attributed these visions to the dips in her blood pressure, a certain medication.

But I believed her, understood she was in some ethereal place between the living and those who had already left. And then came the final dreams, her house dreams, when she'd fall asleep and wake up on the other side of the house or the sides of the house would be reversed. These were the dreams that unsettled her because they seemed so real, as if she had gone to sleep in one room, woken up in another on the other side. I never told her this, but I think those houses were the two sides of her, the living and the dead. She was dreaming her transition.

After she died, my father urged me to go back to the house one last time, to take anything I wanted. All I could do was drive by, sit for a moment in my car outside the cream-colored house, the lawn with no trees. My grandmother gone. I had no reason to go inside.

When I write about the places I've lived, I stop dreaming about them. But Kenny comes back, especially if I write something about him. It's as if rearranging the houses in my writing closes them once and for all, but writing about Kenny opens all the doors and windows, and he is there again, looking the way he did years ago, the way I remember him, the way I write him.

I've looked up all of the places I've lived on Google maps, and in every image, the season is not the one that stands out to me, is not the one I have written. The house in Minturn is half hidden by snow, though I never lived there during the winter. The trees on the corner house in Utah are all bare with no traces of leaves in the lawn, though that's the way I always write that house: the leaves on the lawn, still. Or else the shadow of the branches on the snow in the moonlight. My childhood home in Lubbock is now brown, though when we lived there it was a yellowy-cream. There are three cars in the drive and one parked out front. When I think of the driveway, there's a 1974 orange VW bug parked on the left side. Where, in the image, is the eight-year-old me walking up and down the sidewalk? My white Ford Escape is parked at the corner of North Duncan and Hall of Fame in Still-water, and my bedroom window is open, something I did every morning so our cat could sit and look out. It's as if we're still living there. But we haven't for over a year. I traded in the Escape long before we moved, and I found the cat run over one morning in the middle of the street.

I cannot see the sidewalk to the side entrance of our base-ment apartment in Fort Collins. The angle of the photo only shows the front porch of the house. No matter, I can still see it all: the wind chime, the crack in the bedroom ceiling, the kitchen window.

The third-story apartment in Boulder is rich in sunlight, a version of that place I do not recognize. I've written that apartment in a storm, in the dark, in the middle of the night; even in my memory, I do not remember the sun. All of these images, photos taken from some satellite, are like scenes in a dream. They don't look like the houses I lived in, but I know that they are.

When we lived in Stillwater, Indie had a recurring house dream. The ceiling in my closet had an open space that a previous tenant had covered with an uncased pillow. In the dream, a man comes through that opening, and he's carrying a brass knob from my bed in my parents' house. When Indie was very small, she'd pull these brass knobs from each post and play with them. I'm not sure I even knew the knobs could be removed, and I didn't put it together that at some point, she stopped doing it, even stopped going into the room altogether. I assumed she had outgrown it. But after she told me the dream, I realized that the knobs frightened her, because the man in the dream carried them as weapons. I imagine it's unsettling even to dream that a fragment from one house suddenly can appear in another and hold a meaning you never imagined.

I've never owned a house. I've never had a dishwasher, have never altered the color of walls, have never bought a refrigerator. I borrow rooms and the keys to them. But if I had a dream house, it would be made up of all the favorite parts of houses I have known. It would be on a corner, and it would have the built-in glass cabinets from the house in Utah, the ones that framed the fireplace and held all of my books, the balcony from the Fourteenth Street apartment in Lubbock, the sunken living room from my childhood home on Sixty-third and Toledo, the kitchen counter from the duplex on Washington Street, the river that ran in front of the house in Minturn. The windows of the house would open by cranking a lever, and there would be a tree out front with a tire swing like the one I got Indie last week, the one where she spends most of her afternoons spinning. That would be my perfect house.

The perfect story would be different. It would be one in which Kenny has no mention.

———————

Two nights ago, I dreamed I was leaning out the front window. I was so far out I was almost upside down, propping myself up on my elbows, my feet dangling from the window-sill. And then I saw him, Kenny, standing in the driveway leaning against his truck. Not the truck I remembered, but another one that was packed full, and I knew he had come back. I even said it, "You've come back."

I woke up from it, the way I always do when I dream him, but after all these years, instead of saying, "Go away," to the dark, I just go back to sleep. Kenny's presence in my dreams has become like the man who walks by my house. I no longer wonder why he looks back.

After all, it's something we all do, whether we want to or not.

LOST CALLS

There's a pay phone stand in front of Ye Olde Liquors on Main Street, but the phone has been taken out. Every time I pass it, I imagine calls people might have made there: "They're out of Stoli. How about Ketel One?" or "There's, like, a whole wall of wine in there. I have no idea." I invent non–liquor-related phone calls, too: "Mind if I drop by? I'm a couple of blocks away," or "I've got to stop by Price Chopper and get bagels. Then I'll be home." Passing that empty phone stand is like walking by disappearance. A distant year.

When I pass the liquor store, on my way to the sandwich shop next door, someone's always going out, or in, and I hear the bell on its door ring its good-bye, which always sounds like it's meant just for me. On the sidewalk, the stand has been gutted of its pay phone, its purpose. The sad, dangling wire. That's when I imagine other kinds of calls: desperate, impassioned pleas. Please. But those calls seem more memory than imagination, as if I recognize shadows that once lingered on that sidewalk, in front of that store. I invariably envision a man huddling his shoulders into the

rectangular frame, his callused hand gripping the black receiver waiting for someone to pick up. And it's cold. Or
raining. The streets empty. Or full of no one noticing. How
many *ring, ring, ring, ring*s does he listen to before he faces
one of the truths of his life and hangs up? I imagine his head
down as he steps off the curb and into the parking lot where
I walk now.

About a month ago, I was driving along quiet Route 11 when
I pulled over to the shoulder and picked up my phone. Maybe
it was that stretch of highway I had been on for most of the
afternoon. Something in me had to call. Leave the message.
But my cell phone was dead, and the charger was at home,
forty miles away. That should have been the end of it, but it
wasn't. There had been too many years of silence, and I had to
say something. Anything.

I got back on the road and drove a few more miles. Back
in Watertown, I had a salad and a glass of Pinot Grigio for
lunch. Now that I rarely drink, one glass of wine pours everything with a sense of urgency. The gas station was in Phil-
adelphia, New York, and the pay phone was inside. Picking
up the handle, I had to remind myself of a long-distance code
I hadn't used in over a decade. It came right back to me, all
fourteen digits. And then I pressed ten more.

"Your call has been forwarded to an automated voice mes-
saging system. 3XX-9XX-3XXX is unavailable. At the tone,

please record your message. When you are finished recording, you may hang up or press 1 for more options."

Hang up. Hang up, I told myself. *Don't say the words.*

(This is ridiculous. It's not like he's ever coming back.)

The pay phone call I think about the most was one I made in 1999. At the end of a summer night, I stood under the glare of a gas station's lights after driving ten hours from Colorado to Texas. That was the summer I met Kenny, and the same summer I left him to go back to Texas. That night, he told me, "Don't get too absorbed." And I asked what he meant even though I already knew. I lingered in the parking lot of that gas station for a long while, knowing that once I got on the road to my apartment, the connection we made over the summer would be lost. (I did it anyway.)

It took a year before I turned around and got on that stretch of highway back to Colorado. That time, I stood outside a gas station in Avon and put two quarters into a pay phone to tell him I was done with Texas. That phone call was an offering he took for three years before he lost his connection for me and Indie, before he started a new life of his own. When I tried to stop him, he said, "Jill, don't."

My grip on the phone still tight.

I didn't listen to my own words.

I didn't hang up.

I pulled out the napkin I had written on at lunch and read:

*I can't get over you. I need to say that to you. I thought maybe
if I called and said those words, I finally could. Leave.
Because I can't seem to leave you. I haven't lived with anyone
or been with anyone in . . . well, it's been years . . . I can't
stop writing about you. I've written another book about you.
Did you know that I wrote a book about you a few years
ago? I don't know. Maybe it's because I've spent all this time
writing about you. To you. I write to you, do you know that?
{I looked up to see cars passing by.} Maybe it's because I live
with a version of you, or maybe it's the songs that have been
on the radio today, but I wanted to call. To say the words.
Maybe now that I've said them I can do what I need to do.
Because I'm still where you left me. And I need to leave you.*

I placed the receiver back on the silver handle then paid
for a cup of metallic-tasting coffee. The woman behind the
counter kept her eyes to the register. I wondered if she had
heard what I said. (If he ever would.) Settling in at one of the
red booths along the window, I watched more cars whirring
past. I wasn't going anywhere.

Kenny used to call. All the time. At one point, I remember,
too much. From hotel rooms when he was on the road, from
corner pay phones, from the places he lived before we lived
together. After I came back to Texas, I spent months ignoring
him, even when I'd recognize the number on caller ID as the
pay phone across the hall from his apartment in Colorado. I'd
turn the ringer off or the answering machine volume down,

delete his message after hearing his voice. (And he knew it, too.) He knew where to find me. I just didn't want to be found.

————

I got back on Route 11, my words trailing behind me like sparks from a dragging muffler. Kenny either listened to my message, or he heard my voice and hung up. Or he saved it and listens to it now and again, wondering what to do about what it is I said, if anything. Probably nothing. There's no way to know. It may not even be his phone number, the outgoing message a computerized voice. I could have been leaving words for a stranger. (To be honest, I was the stranger when I made that call—the 2003 version of myself, I'd say, someone I don't even know anymore.) It's been weeks. No word.

————

In 2003, instead of leaving frail words on a voice message, I wrote to him when he went away. A postcard. (He said he never got it. If he were being honest, well.) What if those words had been the right ones, the ones that might have turned his truck around, and I could pull him back across that long stretch of highway and disappear all the long distance. The words: *Come home.* He never did.

————

I can't call back all that I've lost because Kenny won't answer the phone. I can only listen to what may be his phone ringing. (And I shouldn't, really, after ten years.) But that long distance between each *ring, ring, ring, ring* reminds me of a blue truck and his wrist curved over the steering wheel. And so much more. But like the silence between those rings, there's nothing there. Maybe there never was.

The presence of his absence began to pull away years ago. And since that recent phone call, the silence has made me face one of the truths of my own life. No matter what words I might write on a postcard or say to him on a phone, none of them will make a dent. Those words are just lost calls.

But in my writing, his presence hums like a dial tone, an insistent, unwavering chord, and the words I write are like the pay phone stands outside that liquor store, those boxes on the walls of gas stations, or that booth in the rain where Lloyd Dobler drips and holds a pen. They call back all that has been lost. They break through disappearance like a sledgehammer, so that nothing's ever really gone.

CHICAGO

2013–2014

■

KITCHEN TABLE: A HISTORY

I thought the refrigerator was a stove. From the pictures the landlady e-mailed of the apartment we'd be renting a few blocks from the University of Chicago campus, we figured out there was a main room, a bathroom with a shower, a kitchen with what was clearly a microwave on the counter, and somewhere, a couple of shelves. Indie and I began packing our house, the house with a front porch, a kitchen with a top shelf of cabinets I couldn't reach, a garage-door opener, two stories, and a backyard extending into woods that Indie liked to disappear into with a backpack and our big dog, Blue. On weekend afternoons, I'd stand at the kitchen sink and watch the two of them from the window. Would it give too much away to tell you now I wish I were still standing there? Seeing Indie and Blue duck behind the pine tree that shouldered the snow in the winter? I'd wait until I couldn't see the straps from Indie's backpack, the jagged stick she'd picked for walking, and the white tip of Blue's tail. Then I'd turn and sit back down at the kitchen table. There, during the writing hours, I kept my laptop next to a folded blue napkin with a cup of coffee or a fountain drink from the gas station on the corner. The table set, as it were. For writing, nothing more.

I bought the table in 2010 at an Antique Mall in Stillwater, Oklahoma, when I was a visiting assistant professor at Oklahoma State University teaching four sections of composition every semester. The price tag on the table—a 1940s white mottled Formica-and-chrome with two blue chairs—read $150. It was the most I had ever spent on a piece of furniture. In our duplex, it was set against the wall in the cramped living room because there was nowhere else for it to go—the kitchen already overcrowded with a narrow counter, a refrigerator, a gas stove, and a stacked washer and dryer. Indie and I joked that only one of us could be in the kitchen at a time, especially if the refrigerator was open. And I couldn't use the oven except in the winter, because anything over 300 degrees lit up all the rooms like a furnace. Maybe the worst thing was the dryer—when it ran, the walls sweat, and our apartment disintegrated into swells of humidity. When the Marine— who'd fix anything for a six-pack of Heineken—hauled the unit from the wall and found at least two years' worth of lint in the vent tunnel, he told me we were lucky it hadn't caught fire. Maybe that wasn't the worst thing. I know it wasn't the worst thing we had coming.

When I started graduate school in my twenties, I gathered furnishings for an apartment from friends and family.

One friend contributed a wooden kitchen table she found in an abandoned house in Texas. It was a narrow drop leaf with carved legs, and I paired two Target chairs with it and moved it to three different cities until I had two master's degrees and a PhD. It was during those years I met Kenny, and after a bunch of back-and-forths, mostly from me, we moved into that basement apartment in Fort Collins, and in the kitchen, he made us chai tea and we split a grapefruit, an English muffin, and conversation every morning. In the evenings when the window above our kitchen table darkened, we'd laugh over bottles of red and marinated chicken or spinach-stuffed pasta shells. Once at that table, he tried to get me to try sushi, but after one bite, I pushed the plate over to his side and got up to make myself a turkey sandwich.

I have always been adventurous in my life—too much so. Too impulsive, and most times, I risk too much for too little reward. I have made many, many people shake their heads. But in the kitchen, I am a different woman.

Men who have loved me have told me my restlessness exhausts them, that I'm not "safe," that they can't be sure I'll stick around. Yet more than anything else, they (we?) struggle against their inability to unloosen my melancholy (how would I write without it?). And they've all left. Kenny was no different. After four years together, he pulled away (or had I already began my slow pull away from us?). One night, months after he left, when the evenings cooled enough for sweatshirts, I lit candles on the wooden table and spooned sweet potatoes and bananas to Indie in her highchair. A CD played on the portable stereo. It was the first time I realized I could make the kitchen table whatever I wanted it to be.

———

After Kenny left, I finished graduate school writing about nothing but him—about us—in an attempt to write him home. I sent him every essay, and I waited. Longer than I should have. I sent words and words and got none in return. It was a tough lesson: to learn the difference between writing my life and the art of writing. I still write about Kenny, but I don't write him as much as the ghost he's become.

The next summer, Indie and I left for Utah. We took few belongings—her nursery furniture, the writing desk I'd had since my second graduate degree, a nightstand, some end tables, and twenty-seven boxes of books. On the day I unpacked, Indie stacked blocks in the living room, and I set the wooden drop leaf table in the kitchen. Then I picked it up and carried it out the back door to the edge of the yard for the trash collector. To me, the kitchen table was Kenny.

I bought a circular white table with blue chairs, but for the three years we lived in that house with the large kitchen and its seafoam counter and glass cabinet doors, I couldn't sit us down to the table for any meal. In my mind, a kitchen table was memory.

A kitchen table was missing.

A kitchen table was being abandoned.

A kitchen table was a ghost.

For three years, Indie and I ate on the living room floor, and sometimes dinner was no more than popcorn. I walked around the kitchen table innumerable times to the pantry, where I'd pass Frank Sinatra in his studio, smoking a cigarette. Hat on head. The blue frame around the large photograph of Frank pulled the kitchen together—the blue of the chairs, the blue of the frame, the blue of Frank's eyes (even though the photograph was black and white). The kitchen was pulled together. I was not.

When we moved from Utah, I gave away all the furniture in the house: Indie's crib, which she had outgrown, a green couch from a thrift store, a futon someone had given me. My writing desk, like me, had finally fallen apart there. And the kitchen table? A man slid it onto a blanket in the back of his truck. I was glad to see it go. I wanted nothing of what had held me in that house. Nothing of the middle-of-the-night me, staring out the window, wineglass in hand, afraid to sit at a kitchen table.

The first time I spoke with our landlady in Chicago, I stood in our kitchen in New York, watching Indie and Blue in the backyard. Indie throwing a tennis ball. Blue running after it. It was difficult to watch while the landlady told me she didn't accept dogs, even though I had already realized that a studio apartment, Chicago—the compression of its streets— was no place for a Blue Bear who loved to run. But there were other factors to consider, such as the rent, the neighborhood, if Indie would be able to walk to school, and whether the apartment would be furnished. It would, the landlady told me. Was there a private entrance to our apartment? There was not. We could enter through the front door of the house and go through the living room, or we could come in through the kitchen. *And you can use the kitchen anytime you want*, she told me. We never did. Not once during the conversation did I think to ask if she rented the other rooms of her house.

On an afternoon in July, the landlady led us down the narrow stairs to the basement and opened the door. One twin bed sat lonely in the room. (Indie would end up sleeping on the mattress on the floor, and I would sleep on an air mattress atop the box spring.) In the kitchen, the stove turned out to be a mini-fridge. The pictures the landlady sent had hidden what was between the fridge and the microwave: a hot plate.

Before we packed one box in New York, Indie and I had long talks about the sacrifices we would both be making. We talked about how the cut in my salary would affect our lives. The friends she'd leave behind. The loss of the neighbors we'd come to love. The downsizing from the two-story house we rented from the university to a studio apartment. Trading the privacy of our home for one we would share with a woman we didn't know. No cable.

In the past three years, I had progressed from an adjunct faculty member to a visiting professor teaching composition courses to teaching only creative writing, a rare teaching load in academia, and now there was the possibility I would be the Writer-in-Residence in a prominent writing program in Chicago, where two of the most accomplished and respected writers in my field were on the faculty. This was the kind of position that could catapult me to a tenure-track job, but even more significant was the chair of the search committee's assurance to me on the phone that the department would be hiring a tenure-track in nonfiction the next year, and I was the one he wanted. And then there was the fact I only had one more year left in my three-year visiting position at the university in New York, so one way or another, we'd be moving again.

One development in our lives perhaps had a stronger effect on the decision than anything. After so many moves, Indie and I were both attuned to the rhythm, and after a year or two in a place, we both felt the urge to spend days at a time on the road getting from where we were to where we'd be next.

As I was putting Indie to bed one night in May, I told her that in the morning when she got up for school, I would toast a bagel for New York or a waffle for Chicago. I stayed up longer than usual that night—knowing that every decision was mine to make but knowing, too, that my decision had consequences for both of us. Ultimately, I realized I had finally earned a position where I could give her what she deserved, and I was proud of myself for that, for the chance to give her more opportunities, a more diverse environment, more culture. When she walked into the kitchen groggy the next morning, there was a waffle on her plate. I'll never forget that, because I thought, *Wait*.

In the coming weeks, as I packed up the house, every time I pulled tape across a box to close it, a voice in my head told me *no, no, no*. I didn't listen to it.

When I think back to the kitchen in New York, I see Indie and Blue from the window. I see the kitchen table in the middle of the room and Frank Sinatra in his frame on the wall. I see my laptop. The snow spilling diagonally from the gray sky. And when I let myself, I see eggs in a bowl on an October morning. Turkey bacon in the microwave. The coffee sputtering to drip. And me, falling like a puppet released from its strings.

The house in New York shivered for us every day after that. And the kitchen and its table remained little more than my writing space. Indie and I ate side by side on the couch, the one we rented along with our beds and a loveseat. On the day we moved out, we placed our pennies.

I put mine on the sill of the kitchen window where I had watched Indie so many times, and she put one in her room. When it came time to place our penny, we put the last one on the front windowsill, where I had seen her climb up the school bus steps in the mornings and down them in the afternoons, and where she had watched Blue be driven away in the back of a stranger's car while I stood on the front porch, doubled over in sobs. Before we walked out the back door for the last time, I stood in the spot in the kitchen where I had collapsed. How close we had come, I thought, to not being here. And how much closer, it seemed, Indie and I now held on to one another. On the day we locked the U-Box and I gave the wave to haul it away, there was one piece of furniture amidst all the boxes: the kitchen table.

When we unloaded our boxes and carried them down to the basement, I put the kitchen table against a wall, and I hung Frank above it. This time, I didn't call Kenny to tell him we had moved. Maybe it was not having any idea where that phone might ring or the fact that he had never held up his end of the court order. Maybe it was the close call in New York or the call I made from that pay phone along Route 11. Whatever it was, I was done.

Every morning, I followed Indie down the street and watched until I saw her long blonde hair turn into the open gate of her school, and then I turned around and went back to the basement, where I set out my blue napkin and my coffee cup. There are spaces in our homes we can simply make or remake, no matter the city, no matter the size. Indie took the tie-dye wall hanging that had covered one of the walls of her room in New York and hung it like a triangle from perpendicular walls to fashion a canopy over her mattress. We called it her "room."

I can delude myself—I often do—but at no mention of her "room" did I forget that my daughter was sleeping on the floor. And maybe by now you've come to know, if you don't already, that for some (most?) writers, writing is a life of austerity and transience. House to house, city to city. But writers or not, we all make do in this life, one way or another.

At night, I'd sit on the floor next to where she sat on her mattress. We'd eat Lean Cuisines or sandwiches, sometimes something as simple as cheese and crackers with fruit. The hot plate never hot, all of my pots and pans still taped up in the storage room on the other side of the basement stairs.

———————

There are dangers that lurk in houses unseen. But some stand right in front of you, a threat. In Chicago, that threat was the man who rented a room on the second floor.

We'd know he was home by the stench of the food he fried on certain nights, when he'd come home after what we assumed was hours, more like a day's worth, of drinking. He'd stomp across the living room floor, pound up the stairs to his room and back to the kitchen. We could hear our landlady trying to talk to him, talk him down, maybe talk him through. We heard his mumbled *uh-huh*s and the sizzle of the oil in the pan. Sometimes I'd worry about our landlady. She seemed to find him charming (or impossible to escape or an antidote to her loneliness), and on those nights, I'd sneak up the stairs and sit on the top one to listen. On the worst nights, he was incoherent and loud, tossing sentences of slurs. I could make out a word or two, nothing more. She'd tire of him and wander up to her bedroom while he stomped up to his room and back down to the kitchen. So many nights, I'd stay awake until I didn't hear him anymore—then I'd sneak upstairs to check that the burner was off.

The smells of someone else cooking can be a comfort, but they can also be a discomfort. I think of young Paul in Willa Cather's "Paul's Case," who suffered "the loathing of a house penetrated by kitchen odors . . . . inescapable." This was me and Indie, burrowed down in the basement, forced to discover a stranger's secret—that a long day of drinking ended with the sizzle of a fry pan and the same foul-smelling dish. But because I understand addiction, because I understand the darkness that can keep a person up at night, I kept quiet. For a while.

———

Every morning in that basement, I'd sit down at the kitchen table in the blue chair facing the living room so I could look out our two small windows. From them, I could see the bird feeders that hung from the tree branches, the ones I kept filled during the long Chicago winter because I liked to watch the birds flit and feed while I wrote.

In dark times, it's the writing that holds me back—like someone gripping me by the arms to keep me from the precipice of *darker*. I pulled my writing chair out so many times in that apartment that the blue cushion gave way, and no superglue would hold it together longer than a day or two. I found a rubber band to keep it in place. Both Indie's and my nerves were just as fragile. And what had begun to hold us together was now tenuous, as we separated from each other as if running and ducking for cover.

One night while we were falling asleep, Indie's voice came soft from the dark: "Can you get us out of here?" And my answer went back across the dark to her: "I promise."

I had already been trying. Not a month into my two-year writer-in-residence position, the chair poked her head into my office to encourage me to go ahead and go on the job market that year. No one would blame me for leaving the position a year early if I were to get a tenure-track job. When I asked if the department would be listing a tenure-track position, she said no—the department was in a transitional phase, and the administration had imposed an indefinite hiring freeze.

So here we were in October. I was, once again, on the job market with application materials at several universities, but nothing came of it. In December, Indie and I got on a train to Texas to visit my parents, and I tried not to think about all the interviews I hadn't been offered. When it came time to board the train to Chicago in January, Indie and I lingered as long as we could beside the tracks. Boarding, we confessed to each other months later, was one of the hardest things either of us has ever done.

The remaining winter months in Chicago pulled forward as slow as a starting train, and the job market stayed quiet. And then in April, my former neighbor and colleague from Canton, New York, sent me an e-mail with a listing for a nonfiction position at a university in New Mexico. It was a visiting position, but he had been assured by a friend in the department that it had already been approved by the administration to go tenure-track the following year. He knew my writing was located mainly in the West and Southwest, particularly in New Mexico. He also knew I had been hoping, for some years, to get Indie closer to Texas so that she could spend more time with her grandparents. Once again, I put my application materials together and sent them off. This was my last shot at getting us out of Chicago.

A month later, during a break in my Advanced workshop, I logged into the computer in the front of the room and opened an e-mail from the department chair in New Mexico. She offered me the position and included a list of classes in the essay—both creative and academic—which meant I would be returning to the composition classes I promised myself I would never teach again after Oklahoma. But some promises we make to ourselves. And some we make to others.

I looked up at my students for a moment, as if they could know my secret, and then I rushed out the room to my office to call a friend. A writer, too, she knew the difficulty of the job market, but more than that, she had been on the phone with me at least once a week since we had moved to Chicago, listening to my struggles and the unwelcome surprises, the decision I regretted, the way I insisted she not comfort me or try to make sense of what didn't. When I shut my office door and told her, she squealed, then cried. "Honey," she said, "this is your way out. But it's more than that; it's your way home." I accepted the job the next day. When I told Indie, we jumped up and down in the space between our beds, relieved. The relief was interrupted.

There are few meals I remember. Probably because I'm not attuned to food as much as I am to the conversation around it. Memories I struggle with, too. But some tastes linger with us long after the check comes or the dishes are cleared by the host. And some moments run in our minds as if they'll always be happening.

Like this one.

Not long before midnight, the man upstairs barrels for the third or fourth time through the living room on his way back to the kitchen. I have no business being upstairs at this hour of his drunkenness, but I find myself turning the corner to the kitchen. He teeters before the stove, a spatula in his hand. The oil sizzles like an eerie warning. Until this night, Indie and I have both kept our distance and our eyes down in the house, and now here he is. And here I am.

"Every night. Every morning. You stomp down those stairs and across this floor."

That's as far as I get before he yells and comes after me, and I run. I race down the stairs, hands on the wall all the way down as if bracing myself. I slam the door. Indie is awake, standing outside her room. He's standing at the top of the stairs. Now he's stomping down and trying to get in the door. He beats on it. Yells threats. He calls me disturbing names no daughter should ever hear her mother called. I dial 911. I forget to say we're in the basement, so when we hear the knock on the front door, we also hear the muffled politeness of the man upstairs and the landlady answering them away. In minutes, he's back at the top of the stairs. Back at the door. Indie runs, and I follow. She opens the pantry door at the end of the kitchen. "Good," I tell her. "Hide." I call 911 again. Four police officers—all male—stand beneath the tree in the front yard and scoff at my plea. One tells me this isn't a police matter—that I need to talk to my landlady. The next morning we do, but all she does is insist I never talk to the man upstairs after he's come home late at night because he's "stressed." The nights of drunk food-frying increase.

———————

After that night, Indie had a little over a month of school left, and I had a week left in my semester. Every time I put the key in the front door lock, I felt the way Paul did when he turned onto Cordelia Street, "the waters close above [my] head." I knew we wouldn't make it unless I did something to put our last days right, to salvage something from the year-long struggle.

I knifed the box labeled *Pots and Pans* and pulled out the small skillet, the only one I have. I grabbed the cutting board, the one I've had since graduate school. And while Indie hung out in the park after school with her friend Livia for as long as she could, I marinated chicken or seasoned some turkey meat while chopping carrots and slicing apples and pouring green beans into a bowl and adding one packet of Sweet'N Low (this, in my cooking, is flair). I moved the oscillating fan onto the kitchen table and turned the hot plate to 5. I pivoted my laptop and chose an episode of *The Office*. And every night for the last month we lived in Chicago, I cooked. I made it an event, and when Indie came downstairs and into our apartment, I had one chicken breast or a turkey burger in the skillet and a plate of appetizers (carrots and ranch, cucumbers and Italian) on her side of the table. She'd sit, crunch, ask which episode I was watching, and I'd flip whatever was in the skillet, then set a slice of provolone or layer some shredded cheddar jack on top in the final minute before the alarm on the microwave dinged. Then we'd move the fan, the laptop, and the blue napkin from the table. And in their place, we'd set one plate on my side, one on hers, and we'd sit down to dinner.

For the past year, we had taken walks around the block at night to unwind, to get away from the man upstairs and to share the best and worst parts of our days. During these last nights, we didn't lose the walks, but we exchanged those parts of our days over dinner while we sat across from each other and ate a meal I had made or one we had made when her friends had other places to be. What we made was never more than three items and five ingredients—we kept it simple and sure. No more mistaking baking power for baking soda. I wanted to get this right.

For so many years after Kenny left us, I saw Indie and me as living alone. In Chicago, I saw that we lived together. And that what we have is enough. Even with all we don't have, with all we have lost, and with all we have had to lose along the way, what we have is each other, and where we have it best is at our kitchen table.

The other day, Indie asked what I am most looking forward to when we get to our new rental house, and I could picture it before she finished the question. The kitchen table, the same one from Oklahoma and New York, and the same one I'll set down in New Mexico. It's the one I'll set for writing and the one I'll set for dinner, where Indie and I will share the best and worst parts of our coming days.

On the afternoon we made our final walk through the basement apartment in Chicago, pennies in hand, Indie disappeared while I stood in the living room and carefully set my penny on one of the windowsills where I had looked out all those writing mornings, where I had tried to write my way outside of where I was and beyond that basement. Indie came back in the room to stand beside me. She told me she put hers in the pantry in hopes that no one would ever have to hide there again. I hugged her, and because she's at least three inches taller than I am now, I ducked my head onto her shoulder and into her long hair. When it came time to place our penny, I left it up to Indie, the way I always do, and she didn't hesitate. "Put it where the kitchen table was," she pointed, "because we had our best times there."

NEW MEXICO

2014

■

HOME

It's the first week of August, and I'm sitting at the counter of Denny's on I-40 in Amarillo, sipping coffee from a plastic cup and waiting for my to-go order, biscuits and gravy for Indie, who's still asleep in Room 105 across the parking lot of the La Quinta. We've got this down, she and I, packing the trunk with our suitcases and her small TV with the DVD player, the lamp, and the sleeping bags—what we will live on and with until the U-Box arrives. In the back-seat, we each have a side—hers piled with her fuzzy pillows and bright blankets, one lime green, one orange, along with an oversized Kermit with a bandage on his right leg from the years when all her stuffed animals had unfortunate in-juries—mine with the small blue cooler that keeps slices of turkey and provolone, cans of Sprite Zero and Diet Dr Pepper, as well as a large bag for chips and nuts and plain bagels. We'll eat these sandwiches for lunch and for dinner. Behind my seat, I have a bag of books and my laptop. We have everything we need.

A few days before we left Chicago, we drove from Hyde Park to Oak Park to see the Hemingway Birthplace Home and Museum. I parked in a garage along North Oak Park Avenue, and we started walking, following the dark green banners hanging from intermittent streetlights: The Hemingway District.

The smiling woman behind the counter hands me the plastic bag, and I pay before walking back across the parking lot to the dark room. Indie's hidden under the covers on her bed, the one furthest from the door she always chooses. It's two hours till checkout, so I let her sleep and take off for the nearest gas station to fill up. When I get back, I take a shower and pack, shuffle the suitcases and cooler back out to the car I've backed up to the door. Indie sits up in bed and eats. She watches *Frasier* while I get everything back in the car. We have been on the road since July 1, when we left Chicago and drove to Marion, Illinois, and then on to Arkadelphia, Arkansas, before stopping to stay at my parents' house for a month to save money. We left Dallas yesterday, and Amarillo is our last stop before Las Vegas, New Mexico.

From the address I had for the Hemingway museum, we had blocks to go. We passed a misspelled Hemmingways' Bistro and The Write Inn and marveled at the manicured lawns, the tree-lined neighborhood, the combination of redbrick apartment buildings and cream houses set back from the street. A quiet neighborhood. Across from the ornate First Baptist Church sat the museum, and we climbed the steps toward its three columns. Inside, I paid the lady at the desk ten dollars for both Indie and me, a ticket that included a tour of the Birthplace Home two blocks north. Inside, we split up and wandered through the exhibit, and while I leaned over a glass case to read Hemingway's high school report cards, Indie took a seat in front of a television blaring a documentary that featured the sister called "Sunny" reminiscing about their childhoods. I finally gave in and stepped toward what I had come for, the World War I–years exhibit with a copy of the letter nurse Agnes von Kurovsky had written to Hemingway in 1919, the one that begins, *I am writing this late at night after a long think by myself, & I am afraid it is going to hurt you.* This is how I was first drawn to Hemingway, a man so devastated by the loss of love as a young man he went on to write her as Catherine Barkley in *A Farewell to Arms* and into "A Very Short Story," among others. As one of his biographers explained, "He wrote about it all of his life."

––––––––––

Indie gets dressed, brushes her teeth, and zips her suitcase, and I balance it on top of mine in the trunk. We both check around the room and the bathroom one last time before I leave the door card on the counter and the room behind us. Indie is already in the car. I duck into my seat and click the seatbelt then check my rearview mirror to make sure I can see over the bags and the blankets and Kermit. After a month of living between Chicago and New Mexico, this is it. Today. I start the car. Before we pull out, I pat Indie's leg and say, "Let's go home."

———

In my twenties, I started reading all of Hemingway's novels and collecting copies of *The Sun Also Rises*. I even turned a small boat into a bookcase for his books. And then I shared Hemingway with Kenny, and he loved his work almost more than I did. He'd read and reread stories then want to talk about them for hours. He even took his favorite, *The Old Man and the Sea*, on the road when he went on jobs. And when I was pregnant and we decided to read books to Indie, we chose *A Moveable Feast* as the first one. During long afternoons, he and I sat on our futon facing each other, taking turns reading chapters aloud.

———

We get on I-40 West and settle into the hours it will take us to cross from Texas to New Mexico and on to Las Vegas. I set the cruise at eighty-two and the radio to the '70s station. Indie stares out her window, taking in the flat expanse of the Llano Estacado splayed out toward the straight line of horizon we can see in every direction. A U-Haul approaches on the other side of the highway, and we both wave and yell out, "Good luck on your move!" It's something we started years ago. Stephen Bishop's "On and On" starts, so I turn it up and we sing our favorite line the loudest, "puts on Sinatra and starts to cry." It's seventy miles to the border, and the exit sign ahead tells us Wildorado is the next town. We imagine how great it would be to live in a town called Wildorado. The wind turbines in the distance churn in slow motion.

Indie and I left the museum and headed right, toward the house. As we counted the addresses leading to 339, Indie grabbed my hand until we saw the wooden sign and the concrete slab with the date, July 21, 1899. Standing in the shade of a tree, Indie took pictures of the house with her phone while I fought tears on the sidewalk.

At Vega, halfway to the Texas and New Mexico border, cumulus clouds spread across a royal blue sky, and we hear the first guitar chords of Fleetwood Mac's "Go Your Own Way." I ask Indie if she wants to hear the story of the middle name I almost gave her. Today she's wearing the Hemingway shirt she picked out at the museum, the one with *The Old Man and Sea* cover on it. She's worn it almost every day since our trip to Oak Park, and as soon as we get unpacked in Las Vegas, I will pull one of my copies of the novel from a box of books, and she will read it in two sittings. I no longer have the small boat after it fell apart during the move from Oklahoma to New York. So much falls away.

Indie straightens up in her seat, asks, "Is this a story about Kenny?" Just this past year, I've started telling her our history, the years we were together, the months before she was born, the hours of her birth. She likes to piece out the stories—not have everything all at once—as if she wants to take as long as possible to put together the other half of a puzzle. So I begin.

"When it came time to choose your middle name," I tell her, "I suggested *Hemingway*, and Kenny immediately said, 'Jill, don't do that to her.'" Indie breaks up in laughter, rocks back and forth in her seat. "Oh, Mom, no," she says, still laughing. Then she stops for a minute, as if imagining what that would have been like. The white dots of the cotton fields on either side of us blur into a series of bright flashes. Indie groans at the thought of what she assumes would have been lifelong embarrassment. "Thanks, Kenny," she says to the road, and then to me: "Thank goodness he didn't let you do that." Now we're both laughing. We're less than thirty miles from the border.

While the tour group huddled into one of the second-story bedrooms, the guide explained how Hemingway stayed away from Oak Park after he left it, and how he had traveled or lived in Spain and Africa and France and Cuba and Key West and finally, Ketchum, Idaho. Indie took a picture of Hemingway's birth certificate, framed on the wall. I had now, I realized, seen his beginning and his end. I couldn't help but recite a line from *The Sun Also Rises* under my breath: "You can't get away from yourself by moving from one place to another. There's nothing to that." As we descended the steps and turned back toward the museum so that Indie could get a T-shirt and I could pick up some postcards, I filled in some parts the guide had left out, and Indie asked questions. As

we made our way down the sidewalk, I still had a catch in
my voice for the man who lost love and wrote about it, again
and again, who ran from place to place all his life, who drank
so much of himself away. Hemingway, I had known for some
time, was a cautionary tale for me—I could mourn the loss
of love and only write about it and move from place to place
trying to outrun memory, or I could choose not to. The day
felt like the right good-bye to Chicago, to so much more.

————————

I always feel something shift when I approach a border, and
perhaps it's because that's where I feel most at home—on some
invisible line between two states, the then and the now, the
before and the after—and I suspect Indie feels a bit of that,
too—between a parent she knows and a parent she doesn't.

An oversized beige RV passes us, and we dream, like we
do every time we see an RV, about the day that will be us,
when we'll live on the road, and I'll have a laptop in the back,
where I'll write why Indie drives us to wherever we want to
go next.

The flat expanse of Texas extends into the lush green plains
of eastern New Mexico. Further on, the landscape shudders
into calderas, lava-capped mesas, and canyons covered in pon-
derosa pine—all against the backdrop of rust-red rocks, the
gray-green of sagebrush, and a sky heavy with thunderheads.
Up ahead, we see a large sign that crosses over the road like a
bright yellow gateway. America's "Ventura Highway" comes
on the station, and I tell Indie that here, the songs we love
and listen to sound better.

"They make more sense here," I say, looking out to silhouettes of elongated plateaus in the distance.

"Mmm." Indie thinks for a moment. "Everything makes more sense here."

Just then, we pass under the large yellow sign. *Welcome to New Mexico. The Land of Enchantment.* I press my palm to the horn and hold it as we cross the border, the way I always do. We whoop. We lean toward the dash and yell, "New Mexico!" We wave our hands in the air.

We are signaling our arrival. We are letting everyone know we're almost home.

EPILOGUE

.

REWRITE

No autobiography tells the whole story. We're always leaving something out. I remember sitting in the recliner in my counselor's office at The Ridge. It was my second or third session, and I had given him permission to phone my mother, to ask what I had been like as a child. My mother's answer: "She was a good student." Surely this is not the whole story.

In a later session, my counselor asked about Kenny. I looked down at the metal drawers of the desk and locked onto one of the handles. I told the briefest version: "We loved each other. We had a child. He went away."

This, of course, is not the whole story.

My counselor shifted in his seat, cleared his throat. Metal drawer. Handle. Hold on. "There seems to still be a lot of sadness there," his words simple. I said, "Yes." We never spoke of it again. I rolled up that part like a piece of paper and tucked it away.

I remember the day my roommate at The Ridge checked out, her oversized Louis Vuitton bags by the door. She left her blanket folded on her nightstand, an empty bottle of conditioner on the shower floor, and a piece of paper at the foot of my bed with these words: *Rewrite your autobiography. But this time, tell the whole story.*

We are not our autobiographies. We write the way we were. Or the way we weren't. Either way, it's fiction.

Here's an autobiography: She left. He did, too.

And then she wrote it down and released it like a red balloon.

ACKNOWLEDGMENTS

Thank you to everyone at Soft Skull Press for all of your hard work and friendly e-mails. Here's to the amazing Dan Smetanka, the extraordinay editor who understood my story better than I did and knew when to call and what to say.

Special thanks to Marcia Aldrich, Georgia Bellas (and dear Mr. Bear), Charles Blackstone (once again, you sent me in the right direction), William Bradley, The Bull and Porter Family, especially Jordan (love love love), Justin Lawrence Daugherty, Sarah Einstein, Steve Edwards, Brian Flota, Hubbell Gardiner, Stephanie Elizondo Griest, David Hicks, B.J. Hollars, Pam Houston, Shaun Hull, Emily Isaacson, David Lazar, Eric LeMay, Jamie May, Sean Prentiss, Mark Slouka and the Slouka family, Tracy Skopek, my parents, Rusty and Martha Jo Talbot, and to all the folks at The Ridge (wherever you are). There are some important people I didn't write about or didn't name—you deserve thanks for who we were, years ago. Indie would like to add The Billmans, Barbara Blackstone, The Huntleys, and Livia, and I agree.

ACKNOWLEDGMENTS

Much appreciation goes to all of my students at Southern Utah University, Boise State University, Oklahoma State University, and a special shout out to the Truth in Nonfiction group at St. Lawrence University.

I never told my grandmother, Elsie Talbot Moore (1914-2009), how much it meant to me that she asked every visit, "Are you still writing, hon?" Yes, I am.

Many of these essays initially appeared in different versions in journals, anthologies, and blogs, including *Ascent, Bring on the Noise: The Best Pop Culture Essays from Barrelhouse, The Collapsar, DIAGRAM, Drinking Diaries, The Fiddleback, Full Grown People, The Normal School, PANK, The Paris Review Daily, The Pinch, Revolution House, The Rumpus, South Loop Review,* and *Writers for Dinner*. Thanks to the supportive editors who published them.

As always, the biggest thank you is for Indie, for your unwavering understanding during the writing hours and for loving the road as much as I do.

We miss you, Blue.